Defined Contribution Decisions

The Education Challenge

Defined Contribution Decisions

The Education Challenge

Paul Hackleman
and Bill Tugaw

International Foundation of Employee Benefit Plans

The opinions expressed in this book are those of the authors.
The International Foundation of Employee Benefit Plans disclaims
responsibility for views expressed and statements made in books
published by the International Foundation.

Edited by Sheila Nero

Copies of this book can be obtained from:
    Publications Department
    International Foundation of Employee Benefit Plans
    18700 West Bluemound Road
    P.O. Box 69
    Brookfield, Wisconsin 53008-0069
    (262) 786-6710, ext. 8240

Payment must accompany order.

Call (888) 334-3327, option 4, for price information or see
www.ifebp.org/bookstore

Published in 2004 by the International Foundation of Employee Benefit Plans, Inc.
©2004. International Foundation of Employee Benefit Plans, Inc.
All rights reserved.
Library of Congress Catalog Card Number: 03-116309
ISBN 0-89154-584-0
Printed in the United States of America

1M-2.04

Dedication

This book is dedicated to:

Rebecca: I am sorry that we could not go with your preferred title
of LNG or my alternative DCB. Ah, freedom of the press!

Nick and Laurel: May you understand two ideals that have driven me
throughout my entire life. The unexamined life is not worth living.
The way to live life fully is to have an unquenchable curiosity
and an inexhaustible passion for the sky above you,
the ground beneath you and everything in between.

Bobbi and Daniel: It goes without saying that
the commitments in business tend to encroach on family
and personal life. Hopefully we have been able
to successfully round it all out. Current times tell well.

> *"Full fathom five thy father lies;*
> *Of his bones are coral made;*
> *Those are pearls that were his eyes:*
> *Nothing of him that doth fade*
> *But doth suffer a sea-change*
> *Into something rich and strange."*
>
> **William Shakespeare**
> **The Tempest**

> *Communiter bona profundere deum est.*
>
> *Benjamin Franklin*

> *You must be the change you wish to see in the world.*
>
> *Mohandas K. Gandhi*

Table of Contents

PART 1. TRADITIONAL ROLE OF EDUCATION
IN DEFERRED COMPENSATION

PART 2. IMPACT OF LEGISLATION
ON EDUCATION RESPONSIBILITIES

PART 3. DECISION-MAKER CHANGES

PART 4. PARTICIPANT EDUCATION

PART 5. APPENDIX

Acknowledgments

The authors would like to thank the following individuals for their contributions to this book.

For **Mary Willett,** former director of the Wisconsin Deferred Compensation Program and currently with Willett Consulting, thank you for your contributions to public sector deferred compensation plans as past president of the National Association of Government Defined Contribution Administrators (NAGDCA) and your evaluation of this book.

For **Susan Devencenzi,** senior deputy city attorney for the City of San Jose, California, thank you for the legal review and the many years of valuable feedback on deferred compensation strategies and opportunities.

For **John LeHockey,** deputy executive director and chief operating officer, School Employees Retirement System of Ohio, thank you for adjusting your schedule so quickly to provide us prompt feedback on our book.

For **Chuck Sklader,** consultant, SST Benefits Consulting, Scottsdale, Arizona, thank you for your review and feedback on both a general basis as well as the detail you provided on asset allocation.

For **Geoff Rothman,** labor relations director, City and County of San Francisco, thank you for your review of this subject matter and its impact on public sector organizations.

For **Dorothy Cociu, RHU,** Advanced Benefit Consulting, Orange County, California, expert ERISA witness for the U.S. Department of Labor, thank you for your thorough review of the ERISA references and material in this book as well as your valuable, insightful feedback.

Foreword

This book was written to address the significant changes that are taking place in education for defined contribution plans. Responsibilities are growing and technology is providing limitless new models to assist plan sponsor decision makers and plan participants in making informed investment choices.

This book provides an overview of the recent critical changes in plan sponsor requirements as a result of legislative and regulatory changes, the emerging opportunities and challenges in developing defined contribution educational strategies and the new models and tools that can inform both decision makers and plan participants.

We think this book has special value for:

Incoming policy makers, administrators and providers—to provide a quick summary of key information on your responsibilities as a defined contribution plan fiduciary, a method of measuring your organization's due diligence in performing its duties and a blueprint for organizing the information provided to your plan participants.

Veteran policy makers and administrators—to identify ways in which you can assess your plan's current performance and practical steps your organization can take to elevate education and improve compliance.

Incoming decision-making committee members—to represent a training tool both for plan requirements and for prospective issues committee members may need to consider and address.

Readers who are less familiar with deferred compensation and defined contribution programs—as a primer, to introduce changing educational requirements in defined contribution plans. Web resources and sample documents have been included to facilitate your improvement of educational services for both yourselves and your plan participants.

Management and union personnel—to underscore the need to place plan objectives and priorities above organizational and labor objectives to assure that the highest priority is to serve the best interests of plan participants and their beneficiaries.

External providers—to represent a summary of key employer issues and challenges regarding their and their plan participants' informational and educational needs as well as an opportunity to assist with the training of personnel new to the defined contribution field generally and the §457 deferred compensation environment specifically.

About the Authors

Paul Hackleman is the benefits manager for San Mateo County, California and a consultant with I.C. Benefits Consulting with 22 years of employee benefit experience. In San Mateo County, he manages the county's $150 million deferred compensation benefit programs.

With I.C. Benefits, Mr. Hackleman consults with public sector employers on benefit strategic planning, benefit designs, contract strategies and automating deferred compensation requests for disclosure (RFDs) and requests for proposals (RFPs) to reduce cost and improve deferred compensation outcomes through improved services. He is a co-trainer at 457 University and Defined Contribution University (DCU). These programs provide comprehensive information to public employers to assure compliance and to develop plans for repositioning the defined contribution benefit in retirement strategies. Mr. Hackleman has worked with numerous states, counties, cities, municipalities and hospitals to identify new opportunities for repositioning their defined contribution plans to meet changing employee and retiree needs and to elevate educational programs for defined contribution retirement benefits.

Mr. Hackleman is a faculty member of the International Foundation of Employee Benefit Plans Certificate of Achievement in Public Plan Policy— Health (CAPPP™) and the Canadian Advanced Trustee Management Standards (ATMS®)—Pension programs. He is also a voting director with the Foundation's Board of Directors and chair of the International Foundation's Public Employees Board. Mr. Hackleman is the co-author of *Public Employee Benefits: From Inquiry to Strategy,* published in May 2000; and co-author of *Deferred Compensation/Defined Contribution: New Rules/New Game for Public and Private Plans,* published in 2001 by the Foundation.

Mr. Hackleman has a master's degree in European intellectual history from the University of Chicago, and a bachelor's degree in political science and history from Callison College, University of the Pacific. He also completed international studies at Bangalore University in India. Mr. Hackleman is a frequent speaker at national conferences on strategic planning and employee benefits. He is a past professor at John F. Kennedy Graduate School in employee benefits.

Bill Tugaw is the president of SST Benefits Consulting & Insurance Services, Inc. d.b.a. SST Benefits Insurance Services of Los Altos, California. He has over 30 years of diversified financial services experience and is currently licensed for life, health, property/casualty and variable annuities, maintaining a Series 6 license with the National Association of Security Dealers.

As an employee benefit plan broker and consultant, Mr. Tugaw primarily serves large employers in both public and private sectors specializing in alternative financing and managed care of benefit plans, workers' compensation and §457 deferred compensation/defined contribution plan consulting.

Mr. Tugaw is a faculty instructor for the International Foundation of Employee Benefit Plans Certificate of Achievement in Public Plan Policy— Health (CAPPP™) in Employer Strategies and Options. He is a co-trainer at 457 University and Defined Contribution University (DCU). Mr. Tugaw also lectures on employee benefits, automated requests for disclosure (RFDs) and requests for proposals (RFPs) for the Professional Development Program of the International Personnel Management Association (IPMA), the Association of California Water Agencies/Joint Powers Insurance Authority (ACWA/JPIA) and the California Association of Joint Powers Authorities (CAJPA).

Active in industry professionalism, education and legislation, he is the past president of the California Association of Health Underwriters (CAHU), past president of the Silicon Valley Association of Health Underwriters (SVAHU) and founding director of the CAHU Charitable Community Foundation. Mr. Tugaw was honored in the 16th edition of *Who's Who in California*. He is a graduate of Arizona State University with a bachelor of science degree in business.

Mr. Tugaw is co-author of *Deferred Compensation/Defined Contribution: New Rules/New Game for Public and Private Plans* published by the International Foundation in 2001.

Introduction

Never before has the need for individual investor education been greater. Never before has the need for plan decision-maker education been more critical.

Plan participants are confronted with a bewildering array of choices and little guidance on how to make informed decisions. Educational opportunities and sophisticated tools are tantalizingly at hand but offer little direct benefit to the vast majority of individuals who increasingly depend on their investment decisions for their retirement livelihood.

Decision makers have increased responsibility and liability but are often little prepared to understand and address the expansion of their fiduciary responsibility and liability. Even when they do understand the significance of recent changes, few resources are available to guide them in their efforts to overhaul their management strategies, organize their tasks and meet, head on, the due diligence responsibilities associated with their decision-making roles.

In the past decade:

- Employers, particularly private sector employers, have **replaced defined benefit plans with defined contribution plans,** thus transferring the primary responsibility for retirement security from employers to employees.

- New **legislative and regulatory changes** have returned responsibility, especially for educating plan participants, to employers who offer defined contribution plans. Legislative and regulatory changes have also explicitly extended private sector, ERISA-like standards to public sector decision-making processes by introducing "trusts" and "trustees" into public sector defined contribution management and commingling, through plan portability, the oversight of qualified and nonqualified plans.

- Employers, especially public sector employers, have continued to offer a perplexingly **large number of investment options** through one or more providers. While the historic practice of offering numerous funds is understandable, the increased complexity associated with numerous and often duplicative fund options will become increasingly onerous for decision makers and individuals alike.

• **Recent incidents of corporate malfeasance** have heightened awareness of industry practices and the importance of diversification but have done little to prompt concrete legislative or plan guidance for investors to reduce overall risk while increasing retirement assets.

• The explosion of **Web-based analytical tools** has introduced powerful, new educational opportunities but the tools are still little utilized and broadly unavailable to many plan participants. Although these tools offer robust mechanisms for decision makers to review their own fund selection and evaluation, their design and utility are little understood.

• The **decrease in the market value of assets** has prompted investors to reduce voluntary contributions, alter retirement strategies or abandon appropriate long-term commitments to diversified and balanced investment portfolios.

The avalanche of these changing market conditions and new mandates makes the historical processes of managing defined contribution plans ineffective. Decision makers have little choice in addressing these trends or complying with these mandates. They have enormous discretion, however, in the strategies they develop and the systems they install.

Decision makers have been unprepared for the new educational requirements these trends necessitate yet the educational strategies they consider and implement will have profound implications for their successful management of plan responsibilities and their stewardship of plan participant education.

Ultimately, the decisions employers make in response to these changes will affect the efficiency and effectiveness of their operations and fundamentally shape the future retirement well-being of the plan participants they serve. The decisions participants make will affect the soundness of their investment portfolios and the quality of their retirement years.

PART 1

Traditional Role of Education in Deferred Compensation

"We are made wise not by the recollection of our past, but by the responsibility for our future."

George Bernard Shaw

Employer Education

A survey of education in the formative years (1970s-1980s) of participant-directed defined contribution (DC) plans discloses, at best, a barren landscape.

Historically, participant education has not been an integral part of DC plans. It is true that providers offered fund prospectus information. This detailed document may have met regulatory requirements but it offered little helpful information to the vast majority of readers with their investment decisions. It provided little or no help in tailoring fund portfolio options to individual risk tolerance, retirement objectives or time horizons. It was provided without any context or understanding of underlying portfolio construction, diversification or investor appropriateness. Like Mark Twain's assessment of civilization, it represented a "limitless multiplication of unnecessary necessaries."

In the contemporary understanding and application of the term, *education* was rarely provided either by the employer or the provider in the early decades of DC plans.

During this period, employer educational objectives were neither an integral part of plans nor an integrated component of overall retirement benefits. Defined benefit (DB) plans occupied center stage both for employers and—where they existed—unions, while DC options were relegated to ancillary benefits.

Early employer DC decision makers often had financial education and experience. They were finance directors, benefits managers or controllers. But they were given little incentive or resources to evaluate fund performance and fees or comparatively analyze options that made optimal sense for participants.

Furthermore, many investment contracts were and in some cases still are presented in a way that makes the underlying fund expenses and fees nearly indeterminable. What information these decision makers did possess, however, was rarely shared in any comprehensive manner with plan participants.

> *In the contemporary understanding and application of the term, education was rarely provided either by the employer or the provider in the early decades of DC plans.*

Historically, employers relied on providers to offer funds that represented some diversity and were attractive to participants. When the current array of options did not meet participant needs, additional investment options were often added for no reason other than the desire of an individual or a small group of individuals to add funds. Little, if any, scrutiny of such factors as fund performance, associated fees, or duplication of existing options was given to new funds by either the employer or the provider. Many plans, which began with a modest number of options, ballooned as "funds du jour" accumulated.

If there was any due diligence performed at all, it was typically confined to communication between employers about fund options, along with a review of participant costs and fees and the general services that providers offered. Few professional organizations or other external resources focused on education in DC plans. As a result, due diligence was rudimentary, minimalist, sometimes even nonexistent.

All this began to change in the 1990s. As private sector employers replaced DB plans with participant-directed DC plans, the importance of providing basic education to participants grew. New start-up companies used potential corporate growth, with associated stock options, as the primary retirement vehicles. Well-established firms substituted hybrid, cash balance or DC plans for their more costly and cumbersome DB plans.

As a result, participants often learned about DC plans in preliminary transitional meetings, as a means of comparing and contrasting DB and DC plan characteristics. The increased communication regarding DC plans did illustrate their benefits and the general value of tax-deferred savings and investment growth. But they rarely exposed participants to any comprehensive strategy for assessing their individual needs or selecting appropriate investment options.

A number of worker trends also reshaped the perception of DC designs:

- Workers began changing jobs with greater frequency within or between organizations in an effort to improve their livelihood. As skill requirements changed with dizzying speed, employers and employees alike understood that burgeoning skill requirements would force workers and employers to change functions, if not jobs, with greater frequency than in the past. Increased mobility undercut the paradigm of lifetime career employment with a single employer and eroded the value, perceived or real, of DB designs.

- Prolific "horror stories" of private sector older workers losing pension benefits on the eve of retirement underscored the abandonment of employer assurances of lifetime commitment followed by guaranteed retirement. With the migration away from DB designs, workers assumed more and more responsibility and liability for their retirement. Increased employee mobility, decreased employer reliability and lack of portability made DB plans less valuable to worker retirement aims.

- The bull market growth of the 1990s whet the appetite of mobile workers to take possession of their retirement assets. Retirement assets were, after all, employee assets. Correctly or not, both public and private sector employees believed they could manage their own investment portfolios more successfully than their employer could. And because assets were held in individual accounts, they could be controlled more easily and transferred more readily from one employer to another.

> *It can hardly be surprising that little attention was given to the overall importance of education in DC retirement planning by employers, providers or individuals.*

Despite these shifts in worker tenure and market growth, the educational framework for DC retirement benefits was limited, often nonexistent. For decades, there has been little or no way for participants, especially those in public sector plans, to decipher the intricacies of plan options, benefits and the impact of contributions to long-term retirement objectives. Few providers ventured to offer educational support or assistance along lines that are increasingly recognizable today.

These characteristics placed early participant-directed DC plans in a forgotten corner. They had little importance and visibility compared to other mainstream benefits like health plans and DB retirement plans. It can hardly be surprising that little attention was given to the overall importance of education in DC retirement planning by employers, providers or individuals.

Provider Education

The absence of early educational strategies in defined contribution (DC) plans does not represent a critique any more than the absence of in-flight meals or movies would for early aviation. The purpose of discussing the absence of early educational strategies is not to rebuke employers or providers but to understand the absence of educational elements in plan design and employer-provider relationships and to suggest, further, that the role of education is still in its infancy, still ready to be defined.

It also is not a criticism of providers, though it is largely true, that their definition of *service* encompassed installation of new plans, development of

> *The absence of early educational strategies in defined contribution (DC) plans does not represent a critique any more than the absence of in-flight meals or movies would for early aviation. The purpose of discussing the absence of early educational strategies is not to rebuke employers or providers but to understand the absence of educational elements in plan design and employer-provider relationships and to suggest, further, that the role of education is still in its infancy, still ready to be defined.*

7

transactional systems support (primarily enrollment, contributions and distributions) and responsiveness to periodic employer-specific requests. Without employer redefinition of service and marketplace competition, this initial definition was appropriate.

Employers could certainly solicit "new employee" education or periodic educational seminars to provide information, especially for enrollment. Providers happily used on-site informational meetings to present market-based information and build overall plan participation and assets. The information provided to attendees might include discussions of fund variations (e.g., objectives, performance, purpose, suitability for the individual) but there was little consideration by employers, providers or participants regarding broad investment strategies or retirement planning and preparation.

Some providers assumed additional responsibility for administrative processes such as hardship withdrawal advice, catch-up information and guidance on domestic relations orders. But because distribution options were irrevocably selected in 457 deferred compensation plans, little attention was paid to retirees after their distribution selection. In fact, retirees often ceased to be core customers despite what they represented as a percentage of total assets.

It is an unnerving miscalculation that retirees continue to be relegated to second-class citizenship even after changes in distribution selection and portability have precipitated migrations from employer to individual plans. Migrations erode employer plan assets with a corresponding adverse impact on economies of scale and overall costs. Migrations often erode individual retiree assets because many individual investment options siphon more funds from retirees through consistently higher individual fees.

The provision of fund prospectus information is still the bedrock of

> *It is an unnerving miscalculation that retirees continue to be relegated to second-class citizenship even after changes in distribution selection and portability have precipitated migrations from employer to individual plans. Migrations erode employer plan assets with a corresponding adverse impact on economies of scale and overall costs. Migrations often erode individual retiree assets because many individual investment options siphon more funds from retirees through consistently higher individual fees.*

most providers' due diligence aims. While that satisfies legal and disclosure requirements, it does little to enlighten participants about fund characteristics or the importance of allocating assets across diverse funds or asset classes of funds to weather volatile market conditions. Larger employers can obtain group informational services because these large meetings offer providers an opportunity to enroll additional members or increase individual contributions; smaller employers are often on their own.

Recent trends suggest that providers are placing more emphasis on education for plan participants but there is still little recognition by employers or providers that public sector decision makers and administrative support personnel must be included in educational strategies to assure they comply with their growing fiduciary responsibilities.

Nonintegration of Retirement Resources

Prior to the 1990s, in many private sector companies and virtually all public sector organizations, defined benefit (DB) plans constituted the primary retirement vehicle.

Private sector employers who began replacing DB plans with participant-directed defined contribution (DC) plans in the 1990s provided sufficient information to inform participants of their rights and responsibilities (both during transition and after) but offered little information to assist participants with investments to assure sufficient retirement resources. The due diligence responsibilities that had shaped DB strategies for selecting, evaluating and monitoring investments were not transplanted to decision makers who oversaw plan options or to individual investors who assumed those responsibilities in DC plans.

In the public sector, where DC plans (457 and grandfathered 401(k) plans for public employers and 403(b) plans for schools) were implemented *in addition* to existing DB plans, little or no effort was made to correlate strategies between primary and supplemental plans that participants could consider in building their retirement resources.

It is an ironic trend in the public sector that participants often invested in passive or fixed accounts even though their DB plan represented the "conservative" portion of their retirement "portfolio."

11

Often, the administration of deferred compensation/DC was handled by personnel other than those managing the DB plan. As a result, there was little or no coordination in messages or linkages between these retirement programs.

It is an ironic trend in the public sector that participants often invested in passive or fixed accounts even though their DB plan represented the "conservative" portion of their retirement "portfolio." Private sector employees have been consistently more aggressive in their fund selection and allocation of assets than their public sector counterparts.

Today's models of a good asset allocation strategy would clearly argue for the reverse. Yet even now, a large percentage of public sector investments are placed in conservative asset categories. Many of those individuals who migrated their contributions to more aggressive asset classes during the robust growth of the 1990s have retrenched and redirected their contributions once again to conservative investments in light of recent market declines.

This lack of integrated retirement strategies extended to nonemployer retirement income sources as well. DC providers often failed to highlight, either by discussion or example, Social Security benefits or any other assets or retirement accounts in retirement planning education. Similarly, where spousal income represented an additional source of contribution and retirement resources, this variable was not addressed or incorporated into an individual's total asset picture to provide a comprehensive overview of potential retirement income. The only way to consider the entire financial situation was to solicit specific financial planning from outside sources.

As a result of the above, DC plans (even for employers who also offered DB plans) were structured as "siloed" benefits, walled off from other retirement benefits. Whatever education was offered did little to capture the entire picture of a person's potential retirement income and therefore did little to reshape the investment strategy within the DC plan accounts.

Even today, when DB retirement systems have begun to build retirement calculators and DC plans have increasingly sophisticated software capability to describe portfolio options, there often is little or no integration of multiple retirement sources in fund selection and investment strategies.

PART 2

Impact of Legislation on Education Responsibilities

"Financial literacy and worker investment education and advice must be the ongoing focus by the Administration and Congress alike."

Rep. Earl Pomeroy, (D-N. Dak.)
2002 National Summit on Retirement Savings

ERISA

Any discussion of the Employee Retirement Income Security Act of 1974 (ERISA) and public employer participant-directed defined contribution (DC) plans must begin with an acknowledgment that ERISA does not apply to public sector plans. Governmental plans are expressly exempt from the fiduciary standards of ERISA. The concepts and principles of ERISA's fiduciary duties and prohibited transactions, however, may be applied to governmental plans through the common law of trusts, the trust laws of the state in which the governmental plan is located, or the employer's plan documents themselves. Courts often look to ERISA for guidance in the interpretation and application of public sector plan requirements.

> *The vast majority of public sector employers offering 457 deferred compensation plans are either unaware of ERISA entirely and/or convinced that it has no applicability to public sector DC plans. While technically correct, this perspective misses ERISA's potential as both a safe harbor and a best practices model.*

The vast majority of public sector employers offering 457 deferred compensation plans are either unaware of ERISA entirely and/or convinced that it has no applicability to public sector DC plans. While technically correct, this perspective misses ERISA's potential as both a *safe harbor* and a *best practices* model.

The purpose of discussing this law is not to suggest it directly applies to public sector plans but to highlight its key characteristics and discuss the issues that should be important to public sector plan decision makers.

For decades, qualified DC plans under Internal Revenue Code (IRC) Section 401(a) and qualified cash or deferred arrangements under IRC Section 401(k) have been required to hold plan assets in trust for the exclusive benefit of the plan participants. These trust requirements applied to private sector and public sector plans alike. With the passage of the Small Business Job Protection Act in 1996, the trust requirement was extended to eligible deferred compensation plans established under IRC Section 457.

The debate about whether trust fiduciary standards and due diligence requirements applied to public sector plans prior to the Small Business Job Protection Act attracts powerful arguments and advocates on both sides. There is a marvelous passage in Shakespeare's *Measure for Measure* where a sister pleads for the life of her brother. He has been sentenced to death for an offense that many others have committed without being punished. The sister wonders how the law, which has not been applied to others, can fairly be applied to her brother. In a famous line, the deputy replies that "the law hath not been dead, though it hath slept." One could easily argue that ERISA-like fiduciary standards for public sector plans have been in a similar slumber.

After passage of the Small Business Job Protection Act, with its trust requirements, neither ignorance nor avoidance of fiduciary responsibility will do. Neither offers much defense against or protection from the liability associated with the expanded role and responsibility that has been imposed on public sector decision makers. The law has clearly awakened.

The Small Business Job Protection Act's very requirement that plan assets of 457 plans must be held in *trust* (trust, annuity or custodial account) unmistakably carries the implication that those who manage the plan or influence its design or operation are *trustees*. Extensive common law practice, statutory provisions like ERISA and trust laws of the various states have defined and etched trustee responsibilities firmly in accepted standards of decision-maker conduct and practice. Who would argue that a different set of standards and requirements would apply to public sector decision makers? Who would expect that the legislature or courts would apply a unique set of standards to public sector decision makers at a time when the legislative trends are clearly moving toward unification and simplification of DC plans?

Individuals who still argue against the rationale of applying ERISA-like standards to public sector plans frankly miss a key point. ERISA was estab-

> *Individuals who still argue against the rationale for applying ERISA-like standards to public sector plans frankly miss a key point. ERISA was established for a specific reason. In essence, it assures that plan actions benefit plan participants. Would anyone disagree that keeping participant best interests in mind for every decision that is made or every action that is taken is somehow misplaced or inappropriate? The focus on minimizing liability exposure covers up the more appropriate objective or consideration of fostering best practices models of behavior for all plan-related activities.*

lished for a specific reason. In essence, it assures that plan sponsor actions benefit plan participants. Would anyone disagree that keeping participant best interests in mind for every decision that is made or every action that is taken is somehow misplaced or inappropriate? The focus on minimizing exposure to liability covers up the more appropriate objective or consideration of fostering *best practices* models of behavior for all plan-related activities.

If ERISA fiduciary and due diligence requirements represent standards public sector decision makers should be aware of and potentially strive for, it is critical that decision makers understand the basic tenets of ERISA and how they govern decision-maker conduct, processes and decisions.

This is especially true since the passage of EGTRRA (Economic Growth and Tax Relief Reconciliation Act of 2001), which enhanced the portability options between and among different plan types. For example, employees may transfer qualified plan funds (401(k), 401(a), 403(b) and IRAs) into 457 plans. Those transferred funds must be maintained in compliance with their applicable regulatory provisions. This demands that public sector decision makers be familiar with ERISA and, in fact, adhere to ERISA standards in their management of those portions of their overall DC plan benefits.

What then, are the critical ERISA standards public sector decision makers need to know and potentially meet (unless higher state standards apply)? Under ERISA, standards established for private sector DC plans, trustee duties and responsibilities represent the highest level of duty known to law. Interestingly, the standards have their roots in much earlier guidelines as articulated by Judge Benjamin Cardozo in 1928: "A trustee is held to something stricter than the morals of the marketplace. Not honesty alone . . . is the stan-

> *Decision makers are held to the standard of assuring that all their actions and, in fact, their decision-making processes, solely benefit plan participants and beneficiaries. What does that mean? And why are decision-making processes so critical to the standard? Alone, the actions a decision-making body takes only inferentially describe its intent. The alignment of actions with written policies and procedures unmistakably describes intent.*

dard of behavior." The judge avowed that it is a "tradition that is unbending and inveterate," and concluded that "uncompromising rigidity" must be used to assure that "the level of conduct for fiduciaries be kept at a level higher than that trodden by the crowd . . . ".

At the core of ERISA is the requirement that decision makers act on behalf of the exclusive interest of plan participants and their beneficiaries. No other allegiance is higher. Decision makers do not serve the employer. They do not represent labor. They cannot benefit other outsiders. And they certainly cannot be self-serving.

Decision makers are held to the standard of assuring that all their actions and, in fact, their *decision-making processes,* solely benefit plan participants and beneficiaries. What does that mean? And why are *decision-making processes* so critical to the standard? Alone, the actions a decision-making body takes only inferentially describe its intent. The alignment of actions with written policies and procedures unmistakably describes intent.

If decision makers must act for the exclusive interest of participants, how specifically is that determined? The term *exclusive benefit* is a rule in ERISA Section 404(a)(1) and also a common law trust term. As stated in 404(a)(1), the rule specifies that "a fiduciary shall discharge his duties with respect to the plan solely in the interest of participants and beneficiaries and for the exclusive purpose of: (1) providing benefits to participants and their beneficiaries, and (2) defraying reasonable expenses of administering the plan."

The latter duty of "defraying reasonable expenses" is rarely discussed or emphasized. Yet it represents a critical additional responsibility. It requires trustee decision makers to demonstrate that they are also considering ways and taking actions to reduce ancillary costs and administrative expenses. Could one argue that large plans that contract with providers who still charge deferred sales or other contingency fees in a marketplace where these are

> *The critical question for employer decision makers that have fiduciary responsibility, whether covered under ERISA or not, is this: Is it reasonable to expect that a plan participant can "exercise control" or make meaningful investment choices without understanding diversification, liquidity, current and future return, risk of loss and opportunity for gain?*

rapidly becoming extinct have not fulfilled their duty in this second category? It merits discussion.

Given the requirements to act exclusively on behalf of the participant or beneficiary and to defray administrative costs, what differentiates DC responsibilities from those that apply to defined benefit (DB) plans? Fiduciary responsibilities for DC plans are different from those for DB plans because of the nature of "participant-directed" investments. As long as participants have control over their investment decisions they have responsibility for the results of their actions. That is not to say, however, that employers are relieved of fiduciary obligations.

The notion that participants must "exercise control" of the investments of their accounts is central to employer avoidance of liability. The regulatory challenge in the early years for the Department of Labor (DOL), in its guidance, was to establish regulations that defined the circumstances under which a participant was considered to have "exercised control" of assets. Part of "exercising control," regulators insisted, is based on the knowledge with which participants are able to make meaningful, informed, self-interested investment decisions.

The critical question for employer decision makers that have fiduciary responsibility, whether covered under ERISA or not, is this: Is it reasonable to expect that a plan participant can "exercise control" or make meaningful investment choices without understanding diversification, liquidity, current and future return, risk of loss and opportunity for gain? What level of education informs participants sufficiently to assure that they can "exercise control"?

Treasury Regulation 2550.404c-1(a)(2)(B) specifies that plan participants must be provided with or have access to sufficient information to make informed decisions in their selection of funds.

The early conundrum for decision makers under ERISA was: If participants receive the level of education that allows them to exercise control and make meaningful decisions, does that employer activity approach providing "investment advice" and re-expose the employer to the same type of fiduciary liability and loss that ERISA's safe harbor provisions were intended to protect?

The tension between education and advice has been a central dilemma under ERISA since its enactment. As will be seen in the section covering Interpretative Bulletin 96-1 (Chapter 2.4), the initial DOL efforts sought to offer assurances to employers by describing in detail the type of education that employers could offer without crossing the line to investment advice.

> *More recent legislation has reinforced the expectation that employers provide ongoing, thoughtful, comprehensive education. It also appears increasingly clear that access to information is not enough. Participants must understand the choices they have. They must be aware of the consequences of their elections if they are to "exercise control" over their investment decisions.*

In 1977, after ERISA but prior to the codification of 401(k), 401(a), 403(b) and 457 plans, DOL issued a regulation that established four basic conditions that were necessary to constitute investment advice.

Investment advice existed if advice was:

• Rendered for a fee or other form of compensation

• Provided on a regular or recurring basis

• Based on a mutual agreement that advice would be offered for the purpose of employee investment decisions

• Provided for and based upon the specific needs of the individuals.

Despite the efforts to distinguish education from advice, many employers were understandably skittish about providing more education than minimally warranted.

It appears apparent, however, that DOL's initial and ongoing expectations were that employers would play a more proactive role in providing information on investments to plan participants. More recent legislation has reinforced the expectation that employers provide ongoing, thoughtful, comprehensive education. It also appears increasingly clear that access to information is not enough. Participants must understand the choices they have. They must be aware of the consequences of their elections if they are to "exercise control" over their investment decisions.

The 19th century English playwright George Bernard Shaw once remarked that the "greatest mistake about communication is the belief that it has been accomplished." Similarly, the gulf between access to information and understanding is little measured and little understood. Without an ongoing commitment to solicit and analyze feedback from participants, how can any employer reasonably assume that education was accomplished or that plan participants understood the information they received?

It is important to emphasize that the issue of education vs. advice still has not been fully resolved. There is an ongoing debate about the content of information that is provided to plan participants. There is an ongoing debate about the relationship between the communicator of information and the other stakeholders (e.g., employers, providers, fund managers, consultants, advisors). There is an ongoing debate about how different media may be used with diverse plan populations to assure that the messages that are sent are the messages that are received and, more importantly, understood. In Homer's Odyssey, Odysseus sails between Sylla (a sea monster) and Charybdis (a whirlpool) against which all passing ships were wrecked. Employers must negotiate a similar difficult passage in their efforts to balance the need to provide education and avoid the liability of providing advice.

In recent years, the line between investment education and specific investment advice has narrowed considerably. It is safe to say, however, that educational guidance stops short of offering individuals specific fund recommendations for specific allocation of assets in their specific plan. While this trend of expanding education is likely to benefit plan participants in the long run, it poses issues that decision makers must address in the short term to assure that they do not cross the line to investment advice with its corresponding exposure to liability.

Increasingly, a number of neutral, third-party organizations may help resolve the tension between education and advice. These online companies are beginning to contract directly with providers and employers to offer specific investment advice services often through Registered Investment Advisors (RIAs). This approach provides "advice" for the individual participant that takes the investor through an asset allocation recommendation. These new neutral advisors can satisfy the needs average investors have regarding specific fund selection and overall portfolio balance and diversity. Their independence and avoidance of benefiting or profiting from their recommendations balances the liability issues for employers with the educational needs of employees.

If decision makers are to act in the best interests of plan participants and they are expected to determine what education and/or advice is appropriate to provide participants with the ability to exercise control, how does that impact the processes they follow and actions they take? The overarching expectation of plan decision makers and administrators is that they act with prudence and diligence in exercising their fiduciary responsibilities. ERISA Section 404(a)(1)(B) and the common law definition of *trusts* specify that a fiduciary must act "with care, skill, prudence, and diligence under the circumstances then prevailing that a prudent person acting in a like capacity and familiar with such matters would use in the conduct of an enterprise of like character and with like aims." This provision has become known as the *prudent man* or *prudent person* rule.

The prudent person provision of ERISA is the bedrock upon which all actions must be based and taken. It is the yardstick against which actions will be measured. The concept of the prudent person has itself evolved to incorporate still higher requirements that are expected of knowledgeable or informed decision makers. It is perhaps minimally sufficient for decision makers to meet the test of a prudent person but, to the extent that their actions have greater weight, the standards will be higher.

In many cases, the prudent person standards of plan decision makers and administrators have been elevated through common law actions to become a *prudent expert* standard. Essentially, this higher standard either requires decision makers to possess sufficient expertise to carry out directly their responsibilities (e.g., selecting, evaluating and monitoring funds) or to obtain the services of "experts" who can assume those responsibilities and act accordingly.

The action of selecting outside experts does not relieve decision makers of their fiduciary responsibilities. They are still responsible for their selection of outside experts. They must exercise prudence and diligence in that selection. And once an expert has been selected, decision makers must review and understand the information and recommendations outside experts provide. Ultimately, they must be responsible for the decisions they make whether those decisions originate in their own expert analysis and review or rely upon the analysis and review of others. Again and again, common law has upheld the view that fiduciaries cannot fully transfer their responsibility to others.

It is an ironic twist of recent trends that employers that expected to transfer their fiduciary responsibility and associated costs by migrating retirement plans from DB to DC designs were questionably wrong in the early 1980s and 1990s and unarguably wrong today. The increasing focus on DC education, and the more recent trend to incorporate third-party investment advice increasingly bring employers and their retirement plan decision makers back into the picture of direct fiduciary responsibility.

The expectations of "trustees" regarding their fiduciary standards and due diligence requirements represent only part of what public sector employers must understand about the applicability of ERISA-like standards to

> *Employers that expected to transfer their fiduciary responsibility and associated costs by migrating retirement plans from DB to DC designs were questionably wrong in the early 1980s and 1990s and unarguably wrong today. The increasing focus on DC education, and the more recent trend to incorporate third-party investment advice increasingly bring employers and their retirement plan decision makers back into the picture of direct fiduciary responsibility.*

their policies and procedures. The other part of understanding ERISA is being clear about who is covered under the mandates and what actions are subject to the established standards.

There is widespread misunderstanding in public sector organizations about who has fiduciary roles and responsibilities. Oftentimes, organizations assume that the chief political policy-making bodies (e.g., boards or councils) constitute the "trustees" who are solely or ultimately responsible. While it is true that those who exercise final decision-making authority are trustees and do have fiduciary responsibility, the definition of a *fiduciary* is actually much broader and covers a much larger group of individuals in most organizations.

Fiduciaries are identified by the control they exercise over decisions. As a result, fiduciaries exist not only by "title" but also by "conduct." Those who decide or influence decisions regarding selection of providers and investment options are fiduciaries. Those who are responsible for investment monitoring, evaluation and resulting action are fiduciaries. Even those individuals who establish internal or administrative policies and procedures and have the ability to determine exceptions to policies or procedures can be fiduciaries. In short, internal advisory groups, even if they are empowered only to make recommendations to political policy-making bodies, as well as administrative and line staff are all part of the decision-making process and therefore are encompassed within the sphere of fiduciary responsibility.

The determination of fiduciaries is not limited to internal personnel. Third-party contractors who are delegated responsibility through contracts or bundled plan arrangements, and who determine deferred compensation options and provide recordkeeping services are included. Consultants or other advisors who influence fund selection or evaluate fund performance can have fiduciary roles and responsibilities as well.

> *The number of individuals who need to be aware of*
> *fiduciary standards and their roles and responsibilities*
> *in adhering to those standards is much broader than many*
> *public sector employers realize. The implications for this*
> *broader fiduciary group represents the single most*
> *significant change public sector employers face in their*
> *compliance efforts. The educational responsibilities*
> *decision makers have for plan participants is magnified*
> *by the educational responsibilities they have for*
> *themselves and other fiduciaries.*

In general then, the number of individuals who need to be aware of fiduciary standards and their roles and responsibilities in adhering to those standards is much broader than many public sector employers realize. The implications for this broader fiduciary group represent the single most significant change public sector employers face in their compliance efforts. The educational responsibilities decision makers have for plan participants is magnified by the educational responsibilities they have for themselves and other fiduciaries.

Another key area of fiduciary responsibility is important for contemporary decision makers to understand. Fiduciaries are at risk under Section 405(a) and under other trust statutes for the actions of other fiduciaries. This presents innumerable thorny problems for public sector decision-making processes.

For example, it is very common in the public sector for advisory or recommending bodies (committees or ad hoc groups) to do the detailed analysis and then provide a summary of that analysis and recommendations to a political policy-making body. Individuals or subcommittees who perform this analysis preparatory to recommendations to policy-making bodies risk fiduciary liability if those policy-making bodies misunderstand their role and overturn recommendations without reasons based on the best interests of participants. The policy makers, themselves, increase their fiduciary liability with such an action. That is not to say that political policy-making bodies must "rubber stamp" recommendations that come to them. Far from it. But they must be sufficiently aware of their fiduciary responsibility and sufficiently informed of the reasons and justifications for recommendations to take meaningful actions that continue to keep plan participant and beneficiary interests at heart.

As another example, if there are multiple decision makers, such as members of a governing board, a single decision maker who exercises prudent decision making in actions is at risk for liability if another decision maker ignores the interests of plan participants by being uninformed or by paying a higher allegiance to a stakeholder other than the plan participant. In this instance, the other decision makers are at risk for breaching their fiduciary roles based on the actions of other fiduciaries.

> *Fiduciaries are at risk under Section 405(a) and under other trust statutes for the actions of other fiduciaries. If there are multiple decision makers, such as members of a governing board, a single decision maker who exercises prudent decision making in actions is at risk for liability if another decision maker ignores the interests of plan participants by being uninformed or by paying a higher allegiance to a stakeholder other than the plan participant.*

This broad responsibility requires individuals to assure they personally adhere to a high standard. It also requires that they monitor and hold co-fiduciaries to the same high standard when making plan decisions. It is this second responsibility that few employers understand. As will be discussed and demonstrated in the section on decision-maker composition and organization, Chapters 3.1, 3.2 and 3.3, it is increasingly apparent that *all* fiduciaries have responsibility to monitor and police each other. They must assure that processes minimize the likelihood that individuals, whether political policy-making bodies, decision makers or administrative personnel, can operate outside established standards.

The above discussion of common law fiduciary standards as they apply to public sector decision makers is by no means exhaustive. Nor is it intended to omit state requirements, which may be more stringent and require no less familiarity and due diligence adherence. It was intended to provide, however, a practical, abbreviated overview of the areas public sector decision-making trustees must understand and weigh in rethinking the strategies they pursue on behalf of their own educational growth and in the best interests of plan participants. While these provisions are central to any strategic planning, there are numerous other legislative and regulatory changes that have reshaped how employers must manage their responsibilities.

Regulation 2510.404c-1

Although not a legislative act, Regulation 29 CFR 2510.404c-1 (commonly referred to as the 404(c) provisions) established safe harbor conditions under which employers could offer education (that would not expose them to liability) vs. investment advice (that could create potential liability). The employer's exposure to liability was determined by the extent to which participants exercised control over their own investment decisions and the degree to which information was individually-specific and/or investment-specific.

The regulation was first introduced in 1987 as proposed rules for industry representatives and employers to review. It was revised a number of times before final regulations were issued in 1992.

The provision was intended to identify the conditions under which fiduciaries could be relieved of liability for any consequences of employees exercising control over their own investment decisions.

Employers had to meet these basic conditions:

- Offer at least **three diverse investment options** with different risk and return characteristics.

- Provide participants with **discretion over their investment decisions.**

- Allow periodic **investment changes** with a frequency that would permit individuals to deal with market volatility (minimally quarterly).

- Supply **sufficient information about investment options** to allow individuals to make informed decisions regarding their investments and selections.

The first three provisions are easily met by most plans. The last provision, however, raised as many concerns as it satisfied. Does information constitute investment advice? How much information is appropriate? If it is too little, does it risk not meeting the 404(c) provision and corresponding protection? If it is too much, does it risk becoming investment advice with its attached fiduciary liability? For conscientious employers that wanted to meet or even exceed the spirit of educational requirements (i.e., they wanted truly knowledgeable, informed investors), the 404(c) provision perpetuated the ongoing dilemma that employers faced.

Small Business Job Protection Act

The Small Business Job Protection Act of 1996 was a direct legislative response to the Orange County, California bankruptcy filing in December of 1994. Under the prior 457 rules, plan assets were considered general assets of the employer and, therefore, subject to the creditors of the employer in the event of insolvency. The Orange County bankruptcy filing created a crisis that placed individual participant deferred compensation account balances at risk to claimants against the county. In response to the Orange County crisis, Congress expressly sought to assure that all plans avoided any exposed loss of investment by plan participants based on adverse decisions made by the organization. In short, plan participant investments must be protected.

The act actually accomplished many objectives. It explicitly increased the annual 457 plan contribution maximum, which had long been frozen at the level originally established in 1978. It introduced a second opportunity to modify distributions. It afforded, under specified parameters, *de minimis* distributions while participants were still working. It addressed loans (although corresponding regulatory modifications were not made to permit them until resolved in the 2002-2003 regulatory changes). These provisions brought public sector deferred compensation plans closer to their qualified plan counterparts but fell far short of the kinds of changes that would later be enacted by Congress in the Economic Growth and Tax Relief Reconciliation Act of 2001.

The Small Business Job Protection Act's trust provisions, however, did accomplish indirectly what the other provisions did not. Its direct requirement that employers place their deferred compensation plans in a *trust* vehicle (trust, custodial or annuity contract) for the "exclusive benefit of participants or their beneficiaries" mirrored the terms and language long expected of private sector defined contribution (DC) plan trustees under the Employee Retirement Income Security Act of 1974 (ERISA). The message seemed to be clear. Even if many of the deferred compensation provisions mentioned above remained significantly different from private sector requirements, public sector decision makers must adhere to fiduciary standards and due diligence requirements.

Indirectly then, the act constituted the first major legislative signal that public sector nonqualified deferred compensation plans would be brought more in alignment with qualified plans by introducing trust requirements and trustee responsibility.

> *Recognized or not, the impact of the Small Business Job Protection Act was the explicit creation of trusts and trustee requirements for 457 plans of government employers and the less explicit, but no less applicable, extension of ERISA-like fiduciary and due diligence standards to public sector decision makers.*

This connection between the requirement to establish a trust vehicle and the heightened responsibility it introduced for plan decision makers was not immediately clear to all public sector employers.

Few employers saw the act as anything more than a requirement to establish a formal, written trust document.

Few employers interpreted the act to introduce a change in employer fiduciary responsibility with its corresponding exposure to liability.

Fewer employers still, saw any relationship between the act and the level of current education they provided to internal decision makers or plan participants/beneficiaries. The link between fiduciary responsibility and education was still vaguely inferential at best. One can argue that the link is still misunderstood by many plan sponsors today.

Recognized or not, the impact of the Small Business Job Protection Act was the explicit creation of trusts and trustee requirements for 457 plans of government employers and the less explicit, but no less applicable, extension of ERISA-like fiduciary and due diligence standards to public sector decision makers in the deferred compensation arena.

Interpretive Bulletin 96-1

The 1996 release of Interpretive Bulletin 96-1 by the Department of Labor (DOL) constituted an important initial milestone in distinguishing education from investment advice and providing guidance to employers on the educational efforts that could and should be made. It is a vibrant document to this date and well worth decision-maker review on a regular basis.

The bulletin represents to this day an enlightening insight into regulator objectives regarding education. Many of the bulletin's recommendations can and should comprise an explicit centerpiece for employer principles and objectives. As such, numerous general objectives of the bulletin can constitute critical components of any contemporary employer educational strategy.

What are some of the overarching principles of the bulletin? The department clearly wanted to assure that "individual participants and beneficiaries should consider their other assets, income and investments (outside the plan) when applying an asset allocation model or using interactive investment material." As will be seen in the section on new investment advice models, that objective is still largely unfulfilled but no less critical.

The department also expressed its acceptance of combining general retirement principles with specific investment information. It was permissible, the department explained, to furnish "general financial and investment information on estimating future retirement income needs, determining investment time horizons and assessing risk tolerance" linked to specific investments so plan participants could "relate basic retirement planning concepts to their individual situations."

Because the department had commissioned a study by the Employee

Benefit Research Institute (EBRI) prior to the release of the bulletin, the import of the study's findings were also central to department objectives. The study concluded then, as many studies have concluded since, that withdrawals of funds (whether through loans or through lump-sum withdrawals when terminating employment or transitioning from one employer to another) constituted serious threats to retirement savings. Despite these threats, little education was provided to participants about ways these types of actions could significantly undermine retirement savings.

Based on the study, the department recommended that education emphasize the importance of:

- Participating in plans as soon as possible

- Contributing the maximum allowable amount or as much as possible

- Rolling funds into other eligible plans when changing jobs

- Resisting temptations to withdraw funds for other purposes, however compelling.

What employer would disagree that these objectives for plan participants and the responsibility for communicating their importance by the employer are central to the responsibility of decision makers today and in the future?

The reasons for the bulletin were clearly articulated by DOL in its background summary.

"With the growth of participant-directed individual account pension plans, more employees are directing the investment of their pension plan assets and, thereby, assuming more responsibility for ensuring the adequacy of their retirement income. At the same time, there has been an increasing concern on the part of the department, employers and others that many participants may not have a sufficient understanding of the investment principles and strategies to make their own informed investment decisions."

One could easily argue that little has been accomplished in the years since the release of this bulletin to allay the department's concern.

The department's bulletin went on to acknowledge that employers either had not offered programs or had limited the types of programs they offered precisely because of their uncertainty regarding the extent to which these educational efforts crossed the line to investment advice.

Interpretive Bulletin 96-1 was issued with the clear intent to identify "categories of information and materials regarding participant-directed individual account pension plans that do not, in the view of the department, constitute 'investment advice' under the definition of 'fiduciary.' "

> *On the continuum between education and advice,*
> *Interpretive Bulletin 96-1 was the first regulatory effort*
> *to determine how far employers could move*
> *on the continuum without exposing themselves*
> *to unwarranted risk.*

The bulletin was issued after an exposure draft was shared with industry providers and professional organizations.

The bulletin established four categories that represented safe harbors for employers. Employers were not liable if they provided:

1. **Plan information** covering plan benefits, contributions, impact of preretirement withdrawals and the terms or operation of the plan

2. **General financial and investment characteristics** on investment concepts, risk and return, diversification, dollar cost averaging, historical rates of return, effects of inflation and taxes or estimating future retirement needs

3. **Asset allocation models** for all plan participants including sample portfolios or hypothetical scenarios using generally accepted investment theories

4. **Interactive investment materials** including worksheets/software for purposes of estimating future retirement income needs and assessing the impact of different asset allocations on retirement income.

Each of the above four categories could constitute financial advice and exposure to liability if employers went beyond general information and provided plan and participant-specific recommendations that led directly to investment selection.

On the continuum between education and advice, Interpretive Bulletin 96-1 was the first regulatory effort to determine how far employers could move on the continuum without exposing themselves to unwarranted risk. A visual highlight of this continuum is provided in Figure 1.

Figure 1

PARTICIPANT EDUCATION CONTINUUM

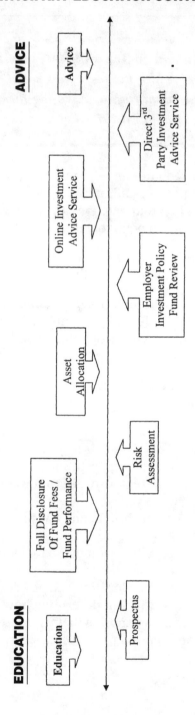

Defined Contribution Decisions: The Education Challenge

Economic Growth and
Tax Relief Reconciliation Act

The broad features of the Economic Growth and Tax Relief Reconciliation Act of 2001 (EGTRRA) are now well known by providers and employers alike. The creation of a specific annual contribution maximum which is consistent among major DC plans (401(k), 403(b), 457) is thoroughly understood as are the annual increases in contribution limits each year to 2006 and the common indexing thereafter.

The portability of funds across qualified and certain nonqualified plans has also received much public attention although neither public sector employers nor employees have been apprised of the importance of understanding the differences in each of these plans, especially since qualified funds that are transferred into nonqualified funds retain their qualified status characteristics. As such, employers must be thoughtful in communicating plan parameters to individual participants who may have numerous types of plans subject to varying tax treatment and guidelines. Those employers that already offered 401(k) or 401(a) plans perhaps got a head start on understanding how these plans differ and how those differences impact education and communication.

For employers and providers, the act requires the maintenance of separate recordkeeping functions that may have an impact on payroll or pension administration systems.

The potential to add "side-car" or deemed IRAs to nonqualified plans also increases the likelihood that future participants may have qualified and nonqualified funds from multiple sources. This will require clear differentiation by employers to assure appropriate administration as well as communication and education.

> *For participants, the opportunity to combine investments*
> *from multiple employers and multiple plans represents*
> *a clear improvement over pre-EGTRRA options.*
> *For employers, the burden of administering,*
> *communicating and educating plan participants*
> *regarding their options and the consequences of those*
> *options will represent a clear additional responsibility*
> *they have not previously known.*

Given the general increased mobility of the workforce, an increasing percentage of future plan participants is likely to have accounts incorporating multiple types of defined contribution (DC) assets. For participants, the opportunity to combine investments from multiple employers and multiple plans represents a clear improvement over pre-EGTRRA options. For employers, the burden of administering, communicating and educating plan participants regarding their options and the consequences of those options represents a clear additional responsibility they have not previously known. There are also clear cost consequences to these additional responsibilities which many employers have failed to address. As will be seen in Chapter 3.8, employers may want to assess this additional burden when they consider administrative expense funding strategies to assure financial support for executing these responsibilities.

The increase in annual contribution limits, the retention of traditional catch-up provisions, the expansion to include catch-up contributions for those aged 50 and over and the tax credit advantages of lower-salaried employee contributions all make DC plans in general and deferred compensation plans in particular more financially powerful. Each stakeholder now has more opportunity and risk in these plans:

- Employees have greater opportunities to contribute for retirement.

- Employers have a more significant benefit to offer to employees (irrespective of whether they offer a defined benefit plan or match contributions).

- Current providers have more asset growth potential.

- Prospective providers have more reasons to enter the marketplace to compete for plan dollars.

By continuing to align 457 deferred compensation plan characteristics with ERISA-covered qualified plans, EGTRRA further enshrined the responsibilities to manage plans under what is rapidly becoming a core set of fiduciary and due diligence expectations.

Sarbanes-Oxley Act of 2002

The Sarbanes-Oxley Act of 2002 established procedures and notification requirements to plan participants and beneficiaries prior to any blackout period and defined a *blackout period* as "any period greater than 3 consecutive business days" when a plan participant may not make investment changes.

Although targeted to 401(k) plans in the wake of Enron's prohibition against investment changes prior to its bankruptcy and not directly applicable to public sector plans, Sarbanes-Oxley unquestionably offers "best practice" opportunities and possibly offers additional protection to public sector decision makers who seek to act on behalf of participant interests.

The act represents the most recent example of the importance of tracking legislation for any defined contribution requirements because public sector plans may have 401 funds that are subject to the act's requirements. As a result, it is important to understand the basic features of the act.

Specifically, the act requires that:

- A blackout notice must be provided at least 30 calendar days, but no more than 60 calendar days, before the start of the blackout period. If this requirement is not met (e.g., the blackout will happen sooner), an explanation as to why the notice could not be provided must accompany the notice.

- The notification must contain certain content including the reasons for the blackout, a summary of investments that are affected, the beginning and end dates of the blackout, the request that participants consider their investments in light of their inability to take action during the blackout and the contact person who can answer any additional questions.

Labor Regulation 2520.101-3 was issued later in 2002. It provided a model plan notice that could be used to comply with the act's requirements.

> *Public sector decision makers would do well to consider adding Sarbanes-Oxley provisions to their investment policies and requiring adherence to those provisions in their contractual agreements with providers.*

Public sector decision makers would do well to consider adding Sarbanes-Oxley provisions to their investment policy and requiring adherence to those provisions in their contractual agreements with providers.

Where the provisions of the act will be most important is in the transition period from one provider to the next and during periods after fund reviews have indicated that certain funds will be placed on a "watch list," closed or removed.

Prospective Legislation/Issues

It is reasonable to expect continuing legislative change in defined contribution (DC) plans. The increasing importance of individual retirement preparedness and the relationship of individual savings to government-provided retirement benefits will keep DC plan parameters in the legislative forefront for many years to come.

Yogi Berra was right when he said, "It's tough to make predictions, especially about the future." Anticipating legislative change or, more importantly, recommending strategies based on anticipated legislative change is as risky as picking "today's hottest stock." When these authors were writing and publishing *Deferred Compensation/Defined Contribution: New Rules/New Game for Public and Private Plans* the Portman-Cardin legislation had just been introduced for the third time. While there was little doubt that consensus was building toward increased limits and expanded portability, many of the more specific provisions were unclear. Coincidentally, the book anticipated many of the specific changes and was published the week Economic Growth and Tax Relief Reconciliation Act (EGTRRA) was signed into law.

> *Discussing prospective legislation, whether it is eventually passed or not and whether it is amended or not, provides an insight to congressional intent and direction that is important for employers to monitor and evaluate in terms of the impact on their overall benefit objectives and retirement plan design strategies.*

Irrespective of last-minute updates, the content of a book is months "old" on the day of publication. No area in a book like this suffers more than a section on prospective legislation. Nevertheless, discussing prospective legislation, whether it is eventually passed or not and whether it is amended or not, provides an insight to congressional intent and direction that is important for employers to monitor and evaluate in terms of the impact on their overall benefit objectives and retirement plan design strategies.

An important prerequisite in this chapter must be understood. This section is not intended to predict but rather describe general trends and what they may portend for employer decision makers. It will explore questions such as: What significant changes are likely to occur? How are any of these prospective changes likely to impact the way employers manage this benefit? What will be the cost consequences? How will individual or employer responsibilities be changed? These are all worthwhile questions to ask.

In January 2003, President Bush proposed replacing 401(k), 457 and 403(b) plans with new Employer Retirement Savings Plans (ERSAs). The Treasury press release rightly suggested that such a replacement would eliminate "the confusing alphabet soup of different savings accounts." Irrespective of whether the replacement soup is more palatable or marketable, the elimination of 457(b) penalty-free withdrawals before the age of 59½ presents a dilemma in gaining police or fire support as they most often retire early. In those plans that permit nonsafety retirement before the age of 59½ (most notably plans that have a target age of 55 for retirement), other nonsafety personnel might be opposed to the change as well. They would clearly lose important benefits they currently enjoy in the current alphabet soup. Thoughts of the TV sitcom "Seinfeld" phrase, "No soup for you!" come to mind in describing the impact of this proposal on personnel who retire before the age of 59½.

On April 11, 2003 Reps. Rob Portman (R-Ohio) and Benjamin Cardin (D-Md.) introduced their Pension Preservation and Savings Expansion Act of 2003 continuing many of the EGTRRA themes. Although subsequent legislative actions have truncated many features of the proposed legislation, their proposal, as drafted, would:

- Make many EGTRRA provisions permanent (remembering that the provisions in EGTRRA are currently scheduled to sunset at the end of 2010).

- Accelerate 401(k), 403(b), 457 and IRA contribution limits by allowing workers in employer-sponsored salary deferral plans under the age of 50 to save a maximum of $15,000 and employees aged 50 and over to save $20,000. Workers under the age of 50, under the proposed provisions, can save $5,000 in an IRA while those aged 50 and over can save $6,000.

- Improve portability for state and local government entities.

- Continue regulatory simplification and further enhance portability, especially for rollovers or spousal rights to retirement benefits upon divorce.

- Expand the Saver's Credit by increasing single and joint filer eligibility to $30,000 and $60,000, respectively, and increase the credit to 60% of the first $2,000 in contributions.

- Modify the minimum required distribution rules from the age of 70½ to 75.

- Introduce preretirement tax incentives for employer and employee health contributions.

- Reform rules to grant employees rights to diversify stock options.

An important provision of this legislative proposal (and still another signal of further actions to come) is the requirement that the Treasury conduct a study on the effect of market condition volatility on investment losses in DC plans. The study findings are due within a year from the date the bill is enacted. Specifically, the study is intended to determine how market volatility may affect:

- Maintenance or addition of new DC plans

- Types of investment options and distribution variations which might reduce future risk of loss

- How the legislature can lessen future losses in DC plans.

While there are still very few legislative changes as a direct result of the Enron situation or more recent SEC violations, it is clear that Congress will keep Enron and other possible corporate failures that endanger retirement investments in mind when they draft new legislative proposals.

A hardy perennial in the retirement area is the consideration of whether portions of Social Security should be privatized. In essence, such a move would replicate on a national, federal front what has already been developed on the employer front, namely, the transfer of retirement responsibility from an established system to an individually based system where the individual must assume increased responsibility and liability for actions and the consequence of actions.

Although the current market conditions and recent corporate missteps make the prospect of this proposal unlikely in the short term, the adverse demographic forces at work in the Social Security system will continue to place pressure on Congress to consider what types of actions it will take to address its long-term solvency.

Irrespective of any specific legislation that might be passed, there are common themes in congressional efforts that run through various initiatives and general goals. They include:

- Removing **barriers to investor contributions** by continuing to create incentives for individuals, in all kinds of different circumstances, to invest in their retirement

- Permitting employees to **diversify funds** by selling company stock under specified conditions or expanding the breadth of their investment options to avoid serious reductions in retirement savings in any particular market cycle

- Educating employees on the **importance of investing and diversifying** to address retirement objectives and investment stability

- Improving **disclosures** to employees about investment performance and fund or administrative costs

- Providing **investment advice services** even if the services are from the same provider that manages the investments (with provisions of disclosure of any conflict of interest).

Latent in these and other legislative signals is whether Congress will establish baseline guarantees of investments which will ultimately bring DC characteristics back closer to defined benefit requirements or characteristics.

What is clear from these current legislative initiatives is that congressional action will continue to focus on ways to facilitate individual investment in retirement. What is less clear is whether that objective serves to bolster individual efforts to augment existing retirement sources or represents a preliminary step to replace those sources altogether. Congressional actions may be a subtle way, some are convinced, to wean individuals from federal, state or employer retirement guarantees and replace those historic safety net systems with individual investment responsibility.

> *Few would disagree that these risks represent real barriers to successful, individually directed retirement strategies. Few would disagree that the transfer of primary retirement responsibility to individuals demands that they be thoroughly informed of their responsibility and thoroughly educated on the investment strategies they should pursue to save successfully for their retirement. Any objective that transfers responsibility without transferring knowledge and resources cannot hope to be successful.*

There are clear indications that transferring investment responsibility from current systems to individuals is not a unified congressional objective. The second National Summit on Retirement Savings occurred in early 2002. Three summits were mandated by Congress. The core objective of the summits is to identify and proliferate communication and educational strategies for different age groups to maximize retirement savings. At the 2002 National Summit on Retirement Savings, Rep. Earl Pomeroy (D-N. Dak.), a leading voice for changes in retirement plan designs and options, expressed concern that market losses and corporate plan design had introduced new risks. He was concerned about the "risk of not having workplace retirement savings; risk of not saving enough; risk of investing in ways that fail to generate the expected return; risk of spending assets intended for retirement on some other purpose—emergency or otherwise; and increasingly, risk of outliving retirement savings."

Few would disagree that these risks represent real barriers to successful, individually directed retirement strategies. Few would disagree that the transfer of primary retirement responsibility to individuals demands that they be thoroughly informed of their responsibility and thoroughly educated on the investment strategies they should pursue to save successfully for their retirement. **Any objective that transfers responsibility without transferring knowledge and resources cannot hope to be successful.**

PART 3

Decision-Maker
Changes

"The reasonable man adapts himself to the world;
the unreasonable man persists in trying
to adapt the world to himself.
Therefore, all progress depends
on the unreasonable man."

George Bernard Shaw

Development of
Decision-Maker Standards

In the early years of public sector deferred compensation plans, and in small plans to this day, finance or human resource directors often assumed responsibility for the selection and decision-making process for plan selection, fund options and available services. Organizations that sought more participative processes often replaced single individuals with committees. In organizations where labor was present, these committees often reflected labor-management representation to assure that participant interests were well protected.

> *The labor-management structure of decision-making committees (e.g., selection of committee members exclusively or primarily based on their representation of labor or management constituencies) has become obsolete because neither labor nor management representatives may represent labor or management. Their sole responsibility is to plan participants.*

Those organizations that established committees to decide or recommend deferred compensation actions developed processes for selecting representatives from both management and labor. Employer criteria for committee membership ran the spectrum from thoughtful (selecting individuals who possessed financial, legal and contract education and experience) to haphazard (selecting any individuals who were willing to serve irrespective of their educational background or financial/investment experience).

Because fiduciaries must act in the sole interest of plan participants or beneficiaries, they may not, by law, have dual loyalties. This requirement prohibits management or labor decision makers from representing their organization or their union in their defined contribution (DC) decision-making roles. As a result, the labor-management structure of decision-making committees (e.g., selection of committee members exclusively or primarily based on their representation of labor or management constituencies) has become obsolete, or minimally an obstacle, because neither labor nor management representatives may represent labor or management. Their sole responsibility is to plan participants.

At the most fundamental level, there is wisdom in rethinking, from the ground up, what appropriate decision-making structure best serves the interests of plan participants. No doubt, discussions that consider the overhaul of current organized structures are not easily initiated. Years of entrenched roles provide current stakeholders with substantial vested interests in retaining current design. But fiduciary responsibility and liability demand reconsideration.

It is precisely because of the difficulty of persuading incumbent decision makers of the significant changes and their legal ramifications, that internal or external legal counsel is often the best proponent of reconsidering a new structure. The argument has been amply advanced and understood in most legal circles. The Employee Retirement Income Security Act of 1974 (ERISA) fiduciary concepts *do* apply to contemporary public sector decision-making processes. Fiduciary responsibility *is* an expectation of public sector decision makers. Liability exposure *is* increased for employers that take no action. The complexity and import of decision-making processes *has* mushroomed.

Using legal counsel to lead the discussion of revisions to internal decision-making processes has three distinct advantages:

1. Legal compliance and risk avoidance are topics within the realm of advice frequently provided by counsel.

2. Legal advice is often well understood and heeded by political policy-making bodies.

3. The involvement of legal personnel in the initial stages increases the likelihood that internal processes will embody common law fiduciary and due diligence standards.

> *While DB fiduciary responsibilities may be different from and greater than DC responsibilities, they represent both a starting point and a "best practices" model upon which DC decision-maker roles and actions can be based.*

While internal legal counsels may not have developed specific benefits expertise, they often provide direct legal support for internally offered defined benefit (DB) plans and, where that is the case, are therefore generally familiar with ERISA, state and common law provisions. Numerous other resources are appropriate for legal or quasi-legal assistance. Third-party legal counsel, provider legal representatives or professional organizations like the National Association of Government Defined Contribution Administrators (NAGDCA) can all successfully demonstrate the applicability of ERISA-like requirements for public sector decision makers. In fact, it was early legal presentations at NAGDCA conferences that brought the issue of ERISA-like requirements for public sector decision makers to the attention of many employers.

Fortunately, many public sector organizations have applicable processes and protocols near at hand. DB decision-making bodies have thoroughly understood for some time their fiduciary responsibility and its impact on their decision-making actions. While DB fiduciary responsibilities may be different from and greater than DC responsibilities, they represent both a starting point and a "best practices" model upon which DC decision-maker roles and actions can be based.

The following chapters in this part focus on the specific areas where it is prudent for employers to rethink their organizational structures and processes.

Assessing Minimum Entry Qualifications

The changing roles and responsibilities of defined contribution (DC) decision-making bodies require an entirely new process for both selection and education of decision makers. Keep in mind the earlier discussion of the breadth of fiduciary responsibility. It not only governs the individual but extends to all of the fiduciaries. As a result, the continuation or establishment of processes that fail to have all fiduciaries understand their role and responsibilities exposes all fiduciaries to liability.

> *Keep in mind the earlier discussion of the breadth of fiduciary responsibility. It not only governs the individual but extends to all of the fiduciaries. As a result, the continuation or establishment of processes that fail to have all fiduciaries understand their role and responsibilities exposes all fiduciaries to liability.*

Employers that continue to be indifferent to staffing of decision-making bodies and administrative support personnel risk organizational and individual liability. Perhaps as important, such indifference perpetuates substandard employer and provider performance, more costly fund options, less efficient and effective administration and fewer potential enhancements of services in general.

Well-educated decision makers and plan participants are not a matter of happenstance. They are the result of accumulated, conscious commitments by employers to act in the best interests of plan participants and their beneficiaries.

Informed, knowledgeable decision makers must either be *selected* based on their knowledge and skills or *developed* through education to possess the knowledge and skills to meet these new responsibilities. Either way, employers must commit new time and resources where none, or little, were required before. Employers that are unable or unwilling to establish more thoughtful requirements for decision-maker selection will pay a higher price for educational development.

Any selection or educational commitment requires ongoing financial resources. Chapter 3.8 discusses options employers may consider in underwriting the cost of these and other requirements.

Fortunately, many public sector employers can tap internal personnel to bring significant knowledge to decision-making bodies. Employees in positions covering internal finance, auditing, legal and retirement plan administration offer significant knowledge in financial principles, investment review and analysis and compliance with legal and legislative requirements. They are candidates who are likely to meet established criteria for decision-making bodies.

Although not commonplace, some employers have already incorporated external expert personnel in DC decision-making roles. These individuals are outside fund managers, brokers, investment advisors and financial consultants who have been selected/appointed to provide objective support for decision-making processes. They either already understand the importance of recent legislative initiatives or can easily be educated to assume their fiduciary roles.

> *Informed, knowledgeable decision makers must either*
> *be selected based on their knowledge and skills or*
> *developed through education to possess the knowledge*
> *and skills to meet these new responsibilities.*
> *Either way, employers must commit new time*
> *and resources where none, or little, were required before.*
> *Employers that are unable or unwilling to establish*
> *more thoughtful requirements for decision-maker selection*
> *will pay a higher price for educational development.*

In his 17th century satire, *Don Quixote,* Miguel de Cervantes astutely observed, "Time ripens all things. No man is born wise." Irrespective of whether internal or external individuals are considered for decision-making roles, irrespective of whether they enter these decision-making roles with much, or little expertise, it is vital for organizations to reconsider what constitutes the critical knowledge decision makers should have to meet these new responsibilities. It is equally vital to establish processes to assure that they have access to and understand this critical knowledge.

Below and on page 57 is a list of the key knowledge and operational information incoming decision makers should receive and incumbent decision makers should possess. Figure 2 provides a visual of the decision-maker education continuum of information that should be provided.

While internal administrative staff should possess specific operational knowledge of the day-to-day activities, decision makers should have a command of the key features of plan operation. Decision makers should have and understand:

- **Plan documents.** Decision makers should have copies of all relevant formal documents associated with their plan(s). These should include trust documents and any amendments, current contractor or provider agreements for administration, recordkeeping or other plan-specific services, collective bargaining agreements when they address plan benefits or responsibilities, applicable insurance coverage (liability/errors and omission coverage), summary plan descriptions and other brief communication material that is provided to employees and retirees regarding plan documents.

- **Administrative policies and procedures.** Decision makers should have a basic familiarity with eligibility, contribution and distribution processes, the array of forms that are used, how procedures governing ancillary services (e.g., hardship adjudication, catch-up provisions, self-directed brokerage option selection, loan processing, domestic relations order requirements) are handled.

- **Roles and responsibilities.** Decision makers should be aware of fiduciary duties, administrative procedures and expenses, conflict-of-interest provisions, dispute resolution mechanisms, meeting requirements and protocols, and trustee expectations.

- **Investment information and reports.** Decision makers should have copies of the investment policy, summaries of plan demographics (number of participants, funds, amount and percentage of assets per

Figure 2

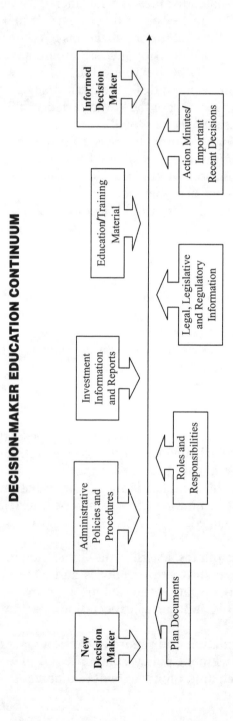

DECISION-MAKER EDUCATION CONTINUUM

Informed Decision Maker

Action Minutes/ Important Recent Decisions

Education/Training Material

Legal, Legislative and Regulatory Information

Investment Information and Reports

Roles and Responsibilities

Administrative Policies and Procedures

Plan Documents

New Decision Maker

funds), copies of actuarial or provider reports, audit reports, recent investment performance reviews and summaries of key past actions decision makers have taken regarding addition and deletion of funds.

- **Legal, legislative and regulatory information.** Decision makers should have a summary of recent legislative changes that have shaped or changed employer plan documents or decision-maker responsibilities. These should also include any legal counsel opinions or comments on plan documents or operation, irrespective of whether that counsel is from the provider, employer or third-party sources.

- **Education/training and material.** Decision makers should have a record of training that has been offered for their training needs and a record of who has attended these programs. Moreover, the education should represent a progression of knowledge and expertise. Decision makers should be able to enter the educational program at any point based on their incoming knowledge and skills.

- **Action minutes/important recent decisions.** Decision makers should have access to recent decisions/actions/policies both as an educational tool for incoming personnel and as a track record for purposes of consistency. The constant interaction between overarching policies and specific decisions or actions should be explicitly understood by all decision makers. Actions that are not consistent with policies represent an area of liability exposure. Policies that have not been revised to incorporate actions represent an area of liability exposure as well.

> *The constant interaction between overarching policies and specific decisions or actions should be explicitly understood by all decision makers. Actions that are not consistent with policies represent an area of liability exposure. Policies that have not been revised to incorporate actions represent an area of liability exposure as well.*

The provision of training to entry-level personnel is critical. Part 5 contains a sample outline identifying the key areas that should be covered with incoming decision makers and administrative personnel. This outline represents only the most basic information and should be quickly augmented with an individual educational plan for each trustee.

Establishing Operational Processes

Chapter 2.1 discussed the basic tenets of the Employee Retirement Income Security Act of 1974 (ERISA) as they have applied to private sector decision makers and the increasing applicability of ERISA-like standards to public sector decision makers. Chapter 3.2 summarized the basic information that incumbent decision makers should possess and the kind of key information that should constitute the training for incoming decision makers. This chapter will focus on what ongoing operational processes should be established.

ERISA identifies the core responsibilities of decision-making bodies. They are: to act in the best interests of plan members and beneficiaries, to offer a variety of investment choices and flexibility in participant selection of choices and to comply with federal, state and regulatory requirements. Beyond these core responsibilities, decision-making bodies need to establish ongoing processes for assuring continual oversight of plan objectives and operations.

Given these responsibilities, what practical standards should decision-making bodies consider or establish for their own conduct? Below are suggested standards in formal plan operation, fund and investment option evaluation and establishment of service standards. A visual layout of these suggested standards is provided in Figure 3.

FORMAL PLAN OPERATION

• **Understand fiduciary responsibilities** by familiarizing decision makers with ERISA and common law expectations as well as any applicable state laws and local ordinances that have been established for trustees.

Figure 3

ESTABLISHING OPERATIONAL PROCESSES

Formal Plan Operation

- Understand fiduciary responsibility
- Assure fiduciaries take responsibility seriously
- Develop, keep current all plan documents
- Maintain current, accurate contracts
- Establish processes for meetings, reviews and action minutes
- Assure uniform, consistent actions.

Fund/Investment Option Evaluation

- Establish fund performance standards
- Determine fund review frequency and process
- Coordinate review with provider(s)
- Develop standards for removal, replacement
- Identify frequency of provider review
- Assure reviews include all fees/costs.

Service Standards

- Establish customer service standards
- Determine employer/participant reports and frequency
- Confirm specific educational services
- Identify exit services
- Assure ongoing survey feedback/analysis.

- **Assure that all operational staff and policy-making bodies understand and take seriously** the established standards.

- **Develop and update plan documents** to assure that all formal requirements are current and that all plan decisions are in accord with the established documents. This means that plans must be reviewed periodically by internal/external legal counsel although provider legal counsel can often make practical recommendations to assure compliance.

- **Maintain current and accurate contracts** to reflect the actual agreements between employer and provider. (This is an area often ignored by many employers.)

- **Establish processes for meetings, reviews and actions** including meeting frequency, attendance requirements, minutes and documentation of actions and expectations for member participation. (This is one of the most basic ways to assure that *all* fiduciaries are acting in a responsible way.)

- **Assure uniform and consistent application of responsibilities** including not only fund and document responsibilities but also the administration of hardship withdrawals, catch-up, domestic relations orders and loans, to name a few.

FUND/INVESTMENT OPTION EVALUATION

- **Establish standards for fund performance review,** ideally including the establishment of an Investment Policy that creates the guidelines by which investment options will be selected, fund performance will be evaluated and decisions will be made.

- **Determine fund review frequency and process** including what funds will be reviewed, what criteria or benchmarks will be used, whether external, neutral or third-party assistance will be required.

- **Coordinate review with providers** to assure that criteria and actions are simultaneously understood and aligned.

- **Develop standards for removal and replacement of funds** to assure that participants and decision makers alike understand how evaluative information will be used to determine core fund options and performance expectations and what explicit processes will assure that underperforming funds are removed.

- **Identify frequency of provider review** for purposes of selecting new providers or recontracting with existing providers.

- **Assure that fund review includes overall fees and other costs** attributed to specific investments or administrative/service costs.

SERVICE STANDARDS

Increasingly, it is important to identify service standards and expectations for providers to assure that plan participants are receiving the educational support they need to make informed decisions. These standards may include the following key areas:

- **Customer service standards** covering phone, voice response system, Internet and print services

- **Reports for both employers and participants** covering specific information, with agreed-upon frequency

- **Educational services** for both decision makers and plan participants

- **Exit services** to assure that upon future potential termination, provider transition responsibilities are completed appropriately and within established agreed-upon timeframes

- **Development of employer-specific surveys** that cover agreed-upon components of service and establish ongoing solicitation of participant feedback and a conduit for employer-provider communication.

Operational processes embed fiduciary responsibilities. They are the means by which policies are fastened to procedures to demonstrate that decision makers understand and take their responsibilities seriously. They are the means by which administrative systems are made explicit and efficient. They are the mechanisms by which decision makers can monitor their decisions and actions.

Combined with standards and decision-maker competencies (discussed in the previous two chapters), they constitute the core of appropriate internal self-governance.

Redefining the
Provider Relationship

The relationship between employers and providers is constantly evolving. Providers consist of recordkeepers, third-party administrators and other companies that offer administrative services as well as various investment product offerings.

Many providers recognize, even if their contracting plan sponsor employers do not, the increased due diligence responsibility for fund selection and monitoring. Many recognize the increasing importance of offering serious, comprehensive, continual education. There is much common ground in the objectives employers and providers have. There is much to gain from aligning employer and provider relationships to secure the objectives both seek.

Employers that take seriously their fiduciary responsibilities invest more time and resources in their interaction with providers than those that practice "hands off" management or those who seek to delegate their responsibility. But ultimately, as mentioned earlier, employers cannot fully delegate their responsibility. They must make a choice. They must select a path. Yogi Berra's decisive suggestion, "When you come to a fork in the road, take it," at least infers that action is firm even if direction is fuzzy. Robert Frost's observation in *The Road Not Taken* is probably more apt. A traveler has a choice of two paths and chooses "the one less traveled by, and that has made all the difference." Employers that fully engage with their providers make a conscious selection of a path to achieving superior outcomes for both themselves and plan participants.

The redefinition of the relationship with providers, however, must overcome years of historical interaction and, in many practical ways, the com-

> *The redefinition of the relationship with providers, however, must overcome years of historical interaction and, in many practical ways, the comfortable inertia of avoiding disruption in one area of benefits when so many other areas of benefits are undergoing such volatile shifts.*

fortable inertia of avoiding disruption in one area of benefits when so many other areas of benefits are undergoing such volatile shifts. This is especially true for employers that contract with multiple providers.

Many employers currently contract with more than a single provider. Employers that have multiple providers do so for a variety of reasons including:

- **Perception of increased competition** between different providers, each of whom would pursue majority share of participants and assets and therefore offer the most competitive funds and services

- **Variation of products** especially related to FDIC-protected options or specific services that different providers feature

- **Stakeholder preferences** often by senior management or participant groups that advocate the addition of providers to serve individual needs

- **Belief that fiduciary responsibilities decrease** when multiple, competing plans are offered.

Precisely because of the legislative and regulatory changes referenced in Part 2, these perceived advantages are diminishing. In fact, they may rapidly become a liability.

> *Because trustee due diligence requirements increase proportionately with the increase in the number of funds requiring review, the use of multiple providers adds complexity without increasing diversity.*

Multiple providers create numerous issues for employers striving for regulatory compliance:

- **Duplicative fund options.** Multiple providers generally offer a similar array of funds within specified asset classes. What really differentiates the various asset classes that competitive providers offer? They often, after all, contract with the same fund families. Other than proprietary funds, most providers today utilize an open architecture that permits them readily to replace one fund with another in any given asset class. Fund performance and fees will admittedly run the gamut from optimal to less competitive within and between providers, but what really makes funds from multiple providers magically superior to competitively selected and managed funds offered by a single provider?

  Because trustee due diligence requirements increase proportionately with the increase in the number of funds requiring review, the use of multiple providers adds complexity without increasing diversity. If the trustee attempts to avoid this additional responsibility by concentrating evaluative processes on funds that have the greatest number of participants and assets, the trustee's inaction on less-utilized fund options (e.g., removal or replacement) increases decision-maker liability. Ignoring evaluative processes on funds that are less utilized by plan participants is not an excuse.

  Ignoring evaluative information on funds that are heavily utilized is equally problematic. It is important to remember that the number of participants or assets in a fund is not an appropriate variable to consider under fiduciary standards. Decision makers that are reluctant to remove underperforming funds because of the size of assets, the number of participants or the fear of disruption do not properly exercise their due diligence. They do not serve the best interests of participants. However difficult it is for decision makers to educate participants on this fundamental responsibility of fiduciaries, it is a task that may not be shirked.

  Rep. Earl Pomeroy (D-North Dakota), speaking at the 2002 National Summit on Retirement Savings, hit the nail right on the head by saying, "In my view, insufficient information is the greatest concern for those facing bewildering investment choices."

- **Reduced economy of scale.** Having multiple providers reduces the economy of scale each provider understandably seeks. The division of assets (e.g., reduction in the ratio between number of participants and assets) reduces the capability of any provider to create optimal net return to participants. The fewer the assets, the more difficult it is for providers to reduce fees or improve services. If there is a direct correlation between size of assets and reduced fees/improved services (and we think there is), then the selection of multiple providers in the absence of compelling reasons to the contrary cannot support employer claims of "acting in the best interests of participants."

- **Increased complexity of administration.** Having multiple providers requires increased trustee intervention to assure alignment of documents, coordination of administrative processes and recordkeeping capability, consistency of communication, education and marketing, fair access and availability. The absence of increased trustee monitoring exposes the trustee to claims of disparity of treatment from either providers or plan participants.

If employers are expected to obtain optimal return for participants through competition and the use of economies of scale, how does that impact the processes of provider selection and contracting?

> *It is important to remember that the number of participants or assets in a fund is not an appropriate variable to consider under fiduciary standards. Decision makers that are reluctant to remove underperforming funds because of the size of assets, the number of participants or the fear of disruption do not properly exercise their due diligence. They do not serve the best interests of participants.*

Our previous book, *Deferred Compensation/Defined Contribution: New Rules/New Game for Public and Private Plans,* discusses at some length the characteristics of request for disclosure (RFD) and request for proposal (RFP) processes. These automated evaluative structures focus on fiduciary responsibility by disclosing which responses best achieve "net return to participants" (fund performance less fund expenses). They anchor provider educational proposals and responsibilities in performance standards/guarantees and contractual language. To summarize briefly, the RFP process should be the chief means by which fund assessment and service performance, particularly educational service performance, are assured. This is accomplished by using the RFP to:

- Subject **fund review processes** to a series of measures that focus on net return to the participant (fund performance less fund fees)

- Balance the needs for **fund diversity and fund manageability** using a process to determine the appropriate number of funds that provide a broad spectrum of fund variation in objectives, style, risk and return without being duplicative

- Disclose **fund fees and administrative costs** to avoid the adverse impact of high costs eroding net return

- Identify **legitimate plan expenses and possible reimbursement** (discussed more fully in Chapter 3.8) that enable employers to support the obligations they have assumed outside of the normal employer budget process

- Determine the specific **educational programs** that will be provided to decision makers and participants throughout the duration of the contract (determining as well their frequency, medium and content)

- Establish the specific **service expectations** covering recordkeeping, reporting, customer service, transition and exit services, all of which are anchored in performance expectations.

The RFD mentioned above is a new term and a new type of automated request. It is a request from the incumbent provider(s) to address the specific and factual fund and service commitments incorporated into existing contractual requirements. It obtains current information on fund returns and current fees. Essentially, RFDs require incumbent providers to attest to the validity of specific fund information, including all fund and administrative costs. Where deferred sales or other contingent charges are assessed, it verifies the specific requirements and aggregate financial liability.

The purpose of the RFD is to establish an accurate, factual baseline of fund, administration and service information against which RFP responses can be compared. It is especially valuable for employers that have not maintained up-to-date contracts. It is also valuable for employers that have not captured through up-to-date reports specific information on fund options, fund costs, number of participants and assets in funds as well as current services. Oftentimes, employer perception of fund characteristics and participation is not in alignment with provider information on funds and participation.

In cases where the employer prefers to recontract with an existing provider, it establishes the factual basis upon which renegotiation of the contract may occur.

For purposes of education, selection and decision making, the RFD also provides the comparison by which all subsequent changes may be assessed and communicated to fiduciaries (especially political policy-making groups) and plan participants.

In short, the RFD may be used in advance of either recontracting or issuing an RFP. Because of its factual, provider-based information, it also provides the baseline assessment of actions decision makers take and verifies whatever due diligence steps have been considered serving the best interests of participants.

> *An employer that has not sampled the marketplace through an RFP process cannot claim with conviction that it has received the best fund and service proposals for its participants through recontracting.*
> *But securing optimal funds and services is precisely what is expected of decision makers.*

As mentioned above, employers may elect to recontract with an existing provider rather than invite responses through an RFP process. The reasons employers pursue recontracting rather than formal RFP processes are understandable. They may create issues of meeting fiduciary standards, but they are understandable.

Recontracting is clearly simpler and less costly than a rigorous RFP process. Employers may have received excellent service from an incumbent. They may be convinced, accurately or not, that they are obtaining the best funds and fees available in the marketplace. On-site service providers may have excellent relationships with plan participants. Employers may be concerned about disruption and the cost of a more deliberative process (although these variables clearly are not part of fiduciary standards).

While recontracting to gain greater efficiencies, better services and lower costs may generate substantial savings to plans and participants alike, it is inherently incapable of producing the same results as an open, competitive process. Even if incumbent providers take seriously the need to repropose services as if an RFP were being conducted, the absence of other proposals makes the outcome murkier and the assertion that optimal funds and services have been secured less confident.

An employer that has not sampled the marketplace through an RFP process cannot claim with conviction that it has received the best fund and service proposals for its participants through recontracting. But securing optimal funds and services is precisely what is expected of decision makers.

The competition for optimal fund performance and service that many employers sought to achieve by contracting with multiple providers is now more appropriately secured through thoughtful RFPs or recontracting and regular (annual) performance audits and evaluations.

The relationship with the provider is not fully defined, however, through the RFP or contracting process. Decision makers cannot pin their hopes of fiduciary compliance on any single activity, even if it has the potential (like RFPs and recontracting do) of establishing the critical assurances for optimal ongoing operation.

Fiduciary compliance is not a "once and done" accomplishment. The RFP or contract can certainly identify ongoing processes and create incentives/disincentives for guaranteeing appropriate outcomes. But trustees must engage in continual due diligence to warrant that standards are being met and performance is occurring as contracted.

Employers have much to gain from redefining their relationship with providers to assure their and plan participants' best interests are met. Providers have much to gain from developing internal capabilities to support this new relationship.

Establishing Performance Standards

Whether performance standards are obtained through requests for proposals (RFPs) or contract negotiations, they express the clear expectation of decision makers regarding the services and commitments that providers make, not just in the area of investment and education but also throughout the relationship of the decision maker and provider.

Guarantees represent a financial anchor or commitment for performance standards and expectations. Guarantees express the consequences of provider failure to achieve mutually agreeable standards. Contracts should therefore include the expectations of provider performance in areas the employer has identified as critical and should include financial penalties or consequences that result when performance standards are not met.

The amount or value of financial guarantees should be significant enough to assure the performance standard. They should not be onerous. It is important to understand that the purpose of financial guarantees is not to collect unexpected revenue. It is to assure the delivery of the agreed-upon standard. In an ideal world, the provider never pays the employer financial guarantees because performance standards have consistently been achieved.

In what areas should an employer seek performance standards and guarantees? Critical areas should include the following general categories and should address the types of questions that are posed for each performance standard.

- **Fund performance expectations.** How are funds evaluated? Are both employer and provider evaluative processes in alignment with commonly accepted standards of performance evaluation and action? How are provider evaluation criteria similar to or different from employer criteria and expectations? How will differences be reconciled (e.g., will neutral third-party evaluators be involved in the process or will internal personnel evaluate provider analysis)? What specific information will be provided to decision makers and with what frequency? Are there established protocols to review fund performance processes and to update and modify fund offerings where appropriate?

> *Although the concept of performance standards is not new, employers have rarely considered or incorporated explicit performance standards and guarantees in defined contribution (DC) contracts despite the fact that they represent the cornerstone of the relationship (contract) between the employer and the provider and the promise or commitment that both parties (employer and provider) make to plan participants.*

- **Processes for managing fund performance review and appropriate actions.** How will fund reports be provided to decision makers? What will be the content of fund reports? How will the results of the review be communicated to policy makers and plan participants?

- **Legal and legislative updates and assurance of compliance in all plan documents and actions.** How will the provider notify the employer of legislative or legal changes that impact plan documents or procedures? Will the provider offer legal analysis to support employer actions and changes to plan documents and procedures or will those services only be available through internal or neutral third-party legal counsel? Within what time frame will notification and recommendations be provided? How will recommendations impact plan documents? How will changes in legal and legislative requirements be reported to stakeholders and who will be responsible for developing and distributing the information? It is important to stress in this area that the provider will qualify his or her advice with the caveat that he or she does not provide legal services. Additionally, the employer should not rely exclusively on the provider's legal counsel as he or she is counsel to the provider and the plan is not the "client." Nevertheless, provider legal counsel can articulate positions that the employer can consider/incorporate into its decision-making processes.

- **Educational requirements for both decision makers and plan participants.** How frequently will decision makers and plan participants receive educational sessions? For plan participants, will education be tailored to active employees as well as retirees? Will education incorporate life-cycle changes as well as specific topics of interest/importance? Will education be available in a variety of media (e.g., print, Internet, computer-based training, distance learning, on-site face-to-face sessions)? Will content be shared with the employer and will the employer have discretion to define information content? How will the number and outcome of educational programs be documented? If so, with what frequency will educational programs be reported?

- **Investment advice services.** Will investment advice services be available? How will investment advice services be promoted, evaluated, monitored and summarized? How will services be financed?

- **Reporting requirements.** With what frequency will reports be available? What plan-level standard and customized reports (ad hoc reporting capability) will be available? How will reports be communicated to decision makers and/or plan participants (e.g., will reports be provided electronically or in print)? Will meetings be provided to discuss report content and import?

- **Customer service expectations.** What phone services will be provided? What hours of operation will be offered? What voice response unit (VRU) services will be available? What Internet services will be available? For all customer services, what standards will be established for access and response time? How will issues/complaints be recorded/addressed/resolved/reported?

- **Transition responsibilities.** What transition services will be expected of a provider who newly assumes business? What services will be expected of an incumbent provider who is being replaced? What special education will be offered to explain changes in fund options and services? Who will be responsible for developing and delivering such training? In what medium and with what frequency will educational/ informational sessions be offered during the transition from incumbent to new provider?

- **Survey and feedback services.** How will plan participant feedback be obtained? Will the provider be responsible for developing, distributing, analyzing and reporting survey results? How will survey results be communicated to plan participants? With what frequency should surveys or other feedback options be offered? Will there be performance standards about the satisfaction levels reported on surveys or feedback systems (e.g., percentage of employees rating satisfaction at 4 or 5 on a 5-point scale)? How will potential or recommended actions based on feedback results be developed, communicated and implemented? How will they be incorporated into contract amendments?

The above areas and questions represent only a beginning for decision makers. The answers to the above questions, however, determine the shape of performance standards.

Additional standards may be appropriate based on specific historical employer experience. For example, if past provider performance has been poor in areas of on-site education, responsiveness to plan participant issues or complaints, timeliness of statements or distributions, any of these areas could be the basis for establishing performance standards and guarantees. Again, the purpose of the performance standards and guarantees is to assure that the provider performs in critical areas to the satisfaction of the employer and plan participants.

Although the concept of performance standards is not new, employers have rarely considered or incorporated explicit performance standards and guarantees in defined contribution (DC) contracts despite the fact that they represent the cornerstone of the relationship (contract) between the employer and the provider and the promise or commitment that both parties (employer and provider) make to plan participants.

> *The use of performance standards is not, however, a one-way agreement. The employer must be able to perform no less than the provider. The employer must commit to measuring and holding the provider accountable. The employer must commit to acting on the information it receives in performance reports. An employer that is incapable or unwilling to act on performance standards reports is no less culpable than a provider who is unwilling to be held accountable. As a result, employer resources are no less influential on outcomes than the provider resources.*

For employers that have not introduced performance standards and guarantees into contracts (whether through a request for proposals or contract renewal process), the desired results may require time. The development of performance standards must reflect the current capability of the provider and employer in articulating, measuring, reporting and acting on the performance standards that are established. Nothing quite so thoroughly undercuts the relationship between provider and employer and their mutual "contract" with plan participants than establishing and then ignoring agreed-upon performance expectations.

Performance standards should legitimately represent a "stretch" for the provider but a realistic stretch. The use of performance standards is not, however, a one-way agreement. The employer must be able to perform no less than the provider. The employer must commit to measuring and holding the provider accountable. The employer must commit to acting on the information it receives in performance reports. An employer that is incapable or unwilling to act on performance standards reports is no less culpable than a provider who is unwilling to be held accountable. As a result, employer resources are no less influential on outcomes than the provider resources.

What then are the characteristics of performance standards and how should they be written? Figure 4 provides a visual highlight of the critical characteristics that well-written performance standards should include.

Minimally, they should include:

• Clear, unambiguous, simple **statements of the performance expectations** anchored to behaviors or measurable activities. The expectations should be observable (e.g., two neutral observers should be capable of independently determining if the performance standard has/has not been met).

• Realistic, **achievable expectations** that are grounded in the provider's existing or prospective operating capabilities. The provider and employer both should constantly assess and reassess the strength of specific services and the ways in which those services can be improved or enhanced. Since this is often evolutionary, both parties should anticipate that contract modifications may be necessary in both the content of expectations and the ways in which those expectations change over time during the life of the contract or relationship.

• Agreed-upon **methods of measuring** performance. This is often the trickiest and most critical component of performance standards. Oftentimes, providers must measure their own performance. While charges of "foxes

Figure 4

CHARACTERISTICS OF GOOD PERFORMANCE STANDARDS

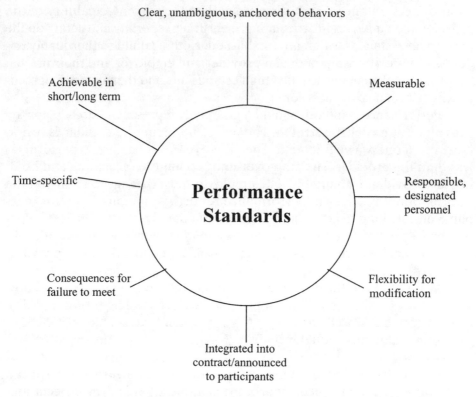

Clear, unambiguous, anchored to behaviors

Achievable in short/long term

Measurable

Time-specific

Performance Standards

Responsible, designated personnel

Consequences for failure to meet

Flexibility for modification

Integrated into contract/announced to participants

guarding the henhouse" may surface, certain important measures must be captured and reported by the provider. Phone response time and turnaround time for transactions are two of many examples where a provider reports information that is difficult or impossible for employers to verify independently. Does that mean they are not worth capturing? Does it mean that the results are not worth evaluating? To both questions, the answer is a resounding "no."

Even those standards that rely on provider review and assessment can be correlated with other standards (like participant satisfaction results) to provide inferential corroboration.

As discussed below, employers can (and should) also clearly articulate the agreed-upon standards to plan participants and expressly invite participants to notify the employer when their individual experience differs from the established standard.

> *No standard should be established without a specific date*
> *at which the standard will be measured and reported.*
> *It is even possible and appropriate to establish*
> *performance standards regarding the measurement*
> *and reporting of performance standards.*

- Specific **time frames in which the performance standard will be expected and reported.** The performance standard should incorporate a single or recurring date in which the outcome will be assessed and/or reported. No standard should be established without a specific date at which the standard will be measured and reported. It is even possible and appropriate to establish performance standards regarding the measurement and reporting of performance standards.

- Identification of **designated personnel** who are responsible for the delivery or reporting of the performance standard. Pinning down the specific individuals who are responsible for delivering and reporting performance alleviates later misunderstanding about the specific process and personnel who are accountable.

- **Consequences of failure to meet the performance standard** both in terms of the financial guarantee and the correction of the performance deficiency. As mentioned above, the ideal outcome is no financial gain for the plan. At best, guarantees should only serve to reinforce the importance of correcting past failures to accomplish mutually agreeable actions or outcomes. Inherent in the reason for establishing performance standards is the objective of establishing processes for correcting underperformance.

- **Flexibility in modifying standards** and guarantees to reflect the results of prior outcomes and the changes in provider capabilities and employer expectations.

Employers are likely to realize the greatest "gains" if performance standards and guarantees are incorporated into formal RFPs (as a condition of obtaining plan business) or through contract renewals (as a condition of retaining plan business). Incorporating standards and guarantees at these times also assures that the provider can consider the amount (cost) of financial

> *Employers are likely to realize the greatest "gains" if performance standards and guarantees are incorporated into formal RFPs (as a condition of obtaining plan business) or through contract renewals (as a condition of retaining plan business). Incorporating standards and guarantees at these times also assures that the provider can consider the amount (cost) of financial guarantees or incentives within the broader, overall context of administrative responsibilities and services established by the contract.*

guarantees or incentives within the broader, overall context of administrative responsibilities and services established by the contract.

Once performance standards have been established, it is critical to communicate them to all stakeholders.

Their communication to policy makers and senior management represents concrete examples of the thoughtfulness to establish them and the means to assure their delivery.

Their communication to plan participants tangibly expresses the focus decision makers have and demonstrates their due diligence. The solicitation of plan participant involvement also helps assure their delivery.

Their communication to providers represents the clear contractual expectations that describe the relationship between the employer and the provider.

Establishing Policies/Procedures

Yogi Berra remarked, "If you don't know where you are going, you may end up someplace else." Like so many of his witticisms, there is an undercurrent of insight. The determination of direction and objectives is central to the success of any decision-making body, including fiduciaries. Policies are the tangible identification of what is important and how actions will be determined and taken.

> *Policies are most effective and "alive" when they are consulted at every decision-point or expected action. As a result, it is important for decision makers to reference policies in their decisions and to cite them when they take actions. It is only through the constant reinforcement of policies, through decisions, actions and communication, that decision makers can demonstrate their efforts to educate plan participants.*

Policies are most effective and "alive" when they are consulted at every decision-point or expected action. As a result, it is important for decision makers to reference policies in their decisions and to cite them when they take actions. It is only through the constant reinforcement of policies, through decisions, actions and communication, that decision makers can demonstrate their efforts to educate plan participants.

What kinds of policies, covering what areas, should decision-making bodies consider? Again, it may be helpful for defined contribution (DC) fiduciaries to look at what their internal defined benefit (DB) boards have assembled in this area. Also, many professional organizations will provide information on policies. Below are some of the critical policies that decision-making bodies should consider and the key characteristics of those policies.

INVESTMENT POLICY

An Investment Policy is perhaps the most important policy statement that decision makers can create because investments are at the heart of DC plans. The Investment Policy is the document that describes to decision makers and plan participants alike the way funds will be selected, evaluated and replaced. Every action taken regarding a fund should be in harmony with the Investment Policy provisions.

What should be the chief components of an Investment Policy? Minimally, they should include:

- A **statement of investment philosophy** that describes the general purpose for which the plan is established. This section should delineate the basic principles of DC investing (risk tolerance, potential rewards, retirement objectives, age and contribution variables). This section may also include the decision maker's executive summary of the number and type of asset classes and funds that are offered to provide a variety of investment choices and sufficient diversity to withstand volatile market conditions.

- **Investment categories** that describe and define each asset class that is offered and that class' specific characteristics and objectives. This section should summarize the types of funds that comprise the category and the chief objectives each fund seeks.

- **Comparison of fund characteristics** is usually provided in a table to facilitate participant comparison of one type of investment with another. Key components should include investment objectives. Types of underlying investments should also be listed. For example, bonds might include "government agency, investment grade, corporate bonds" and mid-cap growth funds may incorporate "common stocks with prospects for growth superior to that of the broad market." Primary source of return, vulnerability to volatility risk and ten-year risk, and the ideal time horizon should be expressed. It may even be valuable and helpful to describe the average participant perception of risk.

> *The investment criteria section of the Investment Policy is often the most critical section to communicate to plan participants when first adopting and communicating the Investment Policy. It should clarify for plan participants the obligations fiduciaries have to review and take action on fund performance. It should make them aware that the specific funds in which they invest may be changed from time to time, based on performance. Plan participants should be encouraged to base their strategies at the asset class, not the fund, level.*

- **Investment selection** categories and processes should be clearly articulated. How will funds be selected? Who will have primary responsibility for selection? Will the provider be initially responsible with the employer decision makers reviewing and approving or will decision makers determine what funds will be offered? If multiple funds are considered for each asset class, what process will be used to winnow funds to the appropriate number as determined by the fiduciaries? How will each of these selection decisions be recorded or documented for later review by decision makers, plan participants or auditors?

- **Standards of investment performance** should explain what benchmarks will be used to evaluate each fund. Many funds can be compared against their "like universe" of funds (as expressed by appropriate rating services specified in the Investment Policy such as Morningstar, Lipper, Russell, Lehman or Ibottson, to mention a few). Other funds (e.g., stable value, asset allocation) do not have easily identifiable benchmarks. In many cases, industry competitors can be used to measure performance.

- **Evaluation criteria** should express the criteria, methodology, frequency and resulting action that will accompany decision-maker review of funds. This section should clearly describe the procedures that decision makers will follow in their process of evaluating funds and taking action for underperforming funds.

    The investment criteria section of the Investment Policy is often the most critical section to communicate to plan participants when first adopting and communicating the Investment Policy. It should clarify for plan participants the obligations fiduciaries have to *review and take action on* fund performance. It should make them aware that the specific funds in which they invest may be changed from time to time, based on performance. Plan participants should be encouraged to base their strategies at the asset class, not the fund, level.

It can also be helpful to correlate the decision makers' scheduled review of funds with the importance of individuals reviewing their funds to determine if there have been changes in risk tolerance, time horizon, retirement objectives or if the portfolio needs to be rebalanced, based on market activity.

- **Disclosure of fees/commissions/charges** should be expressed to assure plan participants that the plan provider has disclosed all charges, fund and/or administrative-specific, related to a specific investment. While nondisclosure may still be rampant in the individual investor market, it clearly has no place within an employer-sponsored plan. Fees are central to determining net return to participants, and participants should absolutely be able to determine from disclosed information the exact fees that correspond to an investment.

- **Prohibitions or limitations** should be enumerated to describe any excluded options or activities. Will the plan allow market timing or selling on margin? Will futures, collaterals, swaps or other cash market instruments be permissible?

- **Communication strategies** should alert participants to scheduled informational releases on decision-maker activities regarding funds. If decision makers wish to include the standards set out in the Sarbanes-Oxley Act, this section would be the appropriate location for informing participants what advance notification will be provided in advance of any actions to permit participants the opportunity to take individual action.

- **Investment education** provides decision makers the opportunity to state plainly what education regarding investment information they intend to impart to plan participants.

- **Investment Policy review** should also be included to communicate to all stakeholders the frequency with which the policy itself will be reviewed and updated or modified. A good example of the importance of periodic review and update is the blackout period provisions in the Sarbanes-Oxley Act, provisions that would not have been contained in investment policies prior to 2002. Similarly, the Morningstar changes in July 2002 have, for many investment policies, modified the star rating (where one star is lowest and five star is highest) methodology for mutual funds they monitor.

For employers that have not adopted an Investment Policy, it is axiomatic to use its development and communication as a restatement of how fiduciaries will fulfill their basic responsibilities.

> *The importance of the Investment Policy as a road map*
> *for decision makers cannot be overstated.*
> *But it also has much broader utility and value.*
> *It is a core component of the relationship between*
> *the provider and employer in their review processes.*
> *It is the core component between the fiduciaries*
> *and those they serve.*

The importance of the Investment Policy as a road map for decision makers cannot be overstated. But it also has much broader utility and value. It is a core component of the relationship between the provider and employer in their review processes. It is the core component between the fiduciaries and those they serve.

As a result, it is important to remember George Bernard Shaw's caution about the greatest mistake of communication being the belief that it has been accomplished. The Investment Policy, perhaps more than any other policy, should be shared and discussed at some length. Below are a few strategies for assuring that the Investment Policy is widely communicated and understood. Decision makers can reference the Investment Policy when they:

- **Develop and implement** it. The initial adoption should be communicated to plan participants with a brief explanation of its key features, especially the ongoing fiduciary requirement of review.

- **Explain any fund modifications** that are made as a result of review. Presentations, print material and other media announcements of changes should expressly mention that actions are taken in accordance with policy provisions and requirements. The communication of fund changes allows trustees to explain why they are taking action (required by the policy), what criteria they used on each fund (as described in the comparison/evaluation sections of the policy), and what the impact is on the participants in terms of fund closure and mapping which refer to both the Investment Policy and Plan Document.

- **Conduct educational sessions** featuring information on processes participants should use to establish their personal investment plan. Let participants know how the plan's selection of investments can correlate to their individual processes for investment selection.

- **Review and modify** the Investment Policy. This is another opportunity to reacquaint current plan participants with and introduce new plan participants to the importance of this document.

- **Enroll participants** in the plan or in new funds. Any eligibility information that is provided should clearly highlight plan documents and specifically the Investment Policy.

EDUCATION POLICY

Few employers expressly state their educational objectives in the form of a policy. With the kinds of changes discussed in Part 2, an Education Policy that encompasses the fiduciary training that will be offered to decision makers allows them to accomplish, simultaneously, several objectives. The policy can cover the kind of training and education expected of fiduciaries. It can disclose the source of that training and its frequency.

It is important to remember that administrative personnel and other stakeholders who are fiduciaries by "conduct" need to be included in any educational considerations. Too often, decision makers establish educational parameters for themselves but fail to consider the kind and frequency of training that must be provided to anyone who has a stake in decisions (and is therefore a fiduciary as discussed in Chapter 2.1).

The Education Policy can communicate the broad participant training objectives (which will be discussed at more length in Part 4). It can provide the important information that is necessary to determine what part of the overall plan budget is allocated to educational efforts and therefore subject to reimbursement.

Like the Investment Policy, the Education Policy can be organized into broad categories that establish the intent of decision makers. Decision makers can choose to have an Education Policy for fiduciaries and/or plan participants. The general provisions of an Education Policy relating to fiduciary training and education can include:

- **Statement of education philosophy** which acknowledges the changing or increasing responsibility of decision makers in fulfilling their fiduciary mandates. It can expressly voice the link between informed, knowledgeable decision makers and appropriate plan actions. It can articulate broad participant educational aims.

- **Basic decision-maker knowledge expectations** and the specific training that entry-level decision makers must complete within a specified period of time. Often, this objective can be achieved either by administrative personnel reviewing their decision-maker material or through the development of a workbook provided to incoming decision makers.

- **Ongoing decision-maker education** that is provided on a scheduled basis. This schedule can be based on trustees' expectations of completing a specified percentage of course credits, or specific conferences or courses decision makers attend. As an example, the International Foundation for Retirement Education (InFRE) has certification programs for both management (Certified Retirement Administrator) and counselors (Certified Retirement Counselor) that offer value to all individuals who have responsibility for this benefit. InFRE sets standards for retirement designations and provides training and testing to ensure that recipients have the necessary competencies to meet their plan responsibilities. The International Foundation of Employee Benefit Plans' CAPPP™ (Certificate of Achievement in Public Plan Policy) pension program is another excellent source for public employee education.

- **Training resources** for provision of educational services. This section can cover those training programs that are conducted internally, those that are secured through contractual arrangements with the provider (through decision-maker educational performance standards and guarantees) and that may be obtained from professional associations/organizations or other third-party sources.

- **Commitment of financial resources** to support the objectives identified above. This section can identify the overall resources that are available and may express the amount of training that will be offered or conducted on a per individual or aggregate basis.

For decision makers who elect to include participant education in their Education Policy, it is important to consider adding another component to those listed above, namely, a Communication Policy to establish the ways in which participant education will be conducted.

COMMUNICATION POLICY

This subsection discusses communication as it relates generally to trustee objectives. This particular medium presents new opportunities for employers to expand their location and deployment of communication strategies.

Yet one could argue that no area of plan management is as important because communication is the glue that binds all other components. Think about it. None of the established decision-maker policies will be as effective if poorly communicated. None of the regulatory requirements and new fiduciary standards will be as well understood if poorly communicated. None of the increasingly robust information/education/investment advice tools will be as useful if poorly communicated.

> *No strategy is complete without precise considerations of how it will be communicated or how its effectiveness (e.g., the degree to which it will be understood) will be measured and assessed.*

If true, why do so many organizations consider communication as an "afterthought" rather than an intrinsic factor in any strategy that is proposed? No strategy is complete without precise considerations of how it will be communicated or how its effectiveness (e.g., the degree to which it will be understood) will be measured and assessed.

The investment of time in developing a comprehensive communication strategy is incredibly well-spent because it makes so many other areas of any strategy efficient. It also has broad applicability to virtually any benefit strategies an employer considers. What are the chief components of a DC Communication Policy? It should include:

- **Assessment of recipient preferences** for receiving information. In Chapter 3.7, we will discuss the new communication media that are expanding opportunities for decision makers to convey important information on an ongoing basis. We also caution readers to consider regularly how their particular plan populace prefers to receive information. If information must be communicated across multiple media, how is that communication coordinated? Is the provision of information in print precisely copied to the Internet, or does the Internet communication have its own organization of content? How do inherent communication strengths in one medium get accomplished in another?

For instance, face-to-face informational/educational sessions typically have an interactive give and take in questions and answers that improves understanding. How will that additional level of understanding be accomplished in print? How will it be accomplished in Web-based communication?

- **Communication objectives** should clearly define how communication will occur for every type of event that occurs. At what times does communication happen? How easily is the medium or media accessed? Should every communication solicit feedback? If so, how will that be incorporated? If not, how will participant review and understanding be determined?

- **Target audience** must be determined for each medium. As will be abundantly clear from the discussion of participant training in Part 4, plan participants are at a variety of places on the information spectrum.

Some employees are new participants, possibly new employees, with little or no basic understanding of DC characteristics or investment advantages. Some are very clear about basic plan parameters but woefully ignorant of fundamental investment strategies.

Some are savvy investors but would benefit from more detailed investment advice based on their career status and proximity to retirement. Some are nearing retirement and need more specialized information on catch-up provisions, review of investments based on near-retirement timelines, etc. Some are in retirement and considering the transfer of funds to individual investment organizations or concerned about stretching investment returns throughout their projected lifespan.

Do these groups need different information at different times? What frequency of information and education is appropriate? What practical limitations do the employer and provider have in terms of addressing divergent participant educational needs? Will media preferences vary depending on the target group?

All of these questions regarding communication objectives and tactics can be answered individually, at the time a specific communication occurs, or they can be addressed comprehensively by considering the entire plan objectives regarding communication and the corresponding strategy for realizing those broad objectives.

> *All of these questions regarding communication objectives and tactics can be answered individually, at the time a specific communication occurs, or they can be addressed comprehensively by considering the entire plan objectives regarding communication and the corresponding strategy for realizing those broad objectives.*

A more comprehensive approach assures that communication is not overlooked. It assures that the connection between any specific action and the basis for that action is understood rather than inferred. It assures that decision makers have a specific means of evaluating their overall educational strategies rather than narrowly focusing on one specific communication.

FIDUCIARY/GOVERNANCE POLICY

The Fiduciary/Governance Policy is intended to summarize the procedures and processes that decision makers follow in their fulfillment of their fiduciary responsibilities. It can be used as an instruction or training tool for incoming decision makers. It can be used as the benchmark by which decision-maker actions are assessed. It can represent a checklist of items that decision makers consider to minimize or avoid liability.

What are the chief components of this policy? The policy should include:

- **Key description of due diligence responsibility** covering definitions, state and common law provisions, state-defined conflict-of-interest provisions, summary of federal and state legislative changes that impact responsibility and recent interpretations or reviews of changing responsibilities

- **Overview of all relevant plan documents** including the formal plan document, contracts, fund options and information on fund activity (e.g., number of participants and funds per asset class, provider policies, key transactional forms, hardship, catch-up and domestic relations order provisions)

- **Decision-maker parameters** incorporating committee composition and structure, staff support, political policy-making bodies and other fiduciaries, decision-making ordinances or processes, decision-maker selection and educational responsibilities and expectations

- **Other employer policies** covering plan benefits. For example, are educational meetings on employer or employee time? May participants use the employer's Internet to access fund information or conduct fund transactions?

- **General expectations of retirement benefit knowledge** covering the employer's other DB or DC plans, service credit requirements or limitations and benefit calculation parameters and tools

- **Communication strategies** covering surveys, feedback systems, method of measuring participant input, processes for incorporating feedback into action plans for modification of policies or processes.

The purpose of describing a variety of policies the employer may consider is not to create a Byzantine structure. Quite the opposite. The more clearly decision makers can articulate to themselves and others the guidelines that shape their decision-making processes, the more efficiently they achieve the objectives they define. Certainly, they must assure that the policies are aligned to avoid any inconsistencies in the processes they develop.

Exploring Web-Based Communication Strategies

Traditional communication has been conducted through face-to-face interaction and print information. New communication media offer enormous possibilities to decision makers. Nevertheless, it is important to reinforce a couple of key points:

- Within most employer situations, there will be a certain portion of the employee population that will not have at work access to e-mail or the Internet. Many employees have occupations that do not require use of personal computers, Internet or e-mail. In many organizations, this can represent as much as a third of workforce personnel. Additionally, employee access may be restricted by employer policies.

    While kiosks and other group access may ameliorate some of the problem, some workers are computer illiterate or have strong preferences for face-to-face receipt of information. As a result, few employers can now currently rely on Internet-only communication. Few employers will ever be able to do so.

    For example, many educational programs and the vast majority of investment advice services are Internet-based. While use of these services will provide an immediate and direct benefit to individuals who have direct access to the Internet (at work or at home) additional employer actions will be required to offer the same benefit (or a similar substitute) to those who do not have or choose not to access this medium.

    How, for instance, will employers make investment advice available to those individuals who do not have Internet access? Are they not the plan participants likely to be in the greatest need of such advice? How will the ready access to plan documents, forms and other Internet content information be replicated for those plan participants who cannot or will not utilize this medium? Decision makers must wrestle with these issues and develop conscious strategies to provide communication across the spectrum of plan participant population.

- As mentioned in the previous section, some plan participants **prefer face-to-face interaction,** individually or in a group. Retirees, as a rule, greatly appreciate individual attention and interaction. They are less likely to avail themselves of Internet options. If access and successful communication/education are the objectives of decision makers, these preferences cannot be ignored or underestimated in strategies.

Although Internet strategies are not a paperless panacea for education and communication objectives, they still represent a large and growing preference by plan participants. As such, they should form an integral part of the overall strategies decision makers consider in their efforts to have plan participants understand the options they have and to "exercise control" over their investment decisions.

New Web capability and utility represent a refreshing advantage for employers and providers alike. They allow both to house important information in a location that is readily available to plan participants around the clock. They increasingly represent inexpensive conduits for employer-provider communication and plan participant feedback. They typically offer improved services at a fraction of previous costs.

If Web sites have ongoing limited utility, how can employers and providers seize this expanding medium and use it to its fullest? And what should the con-

> *Although Internet strategies are not a paperless panacea for education and communication objectives, they still represent a large and growing preference by plan participants. As such, they should form an integral part of the overall strategies decision makers consider in their efforts to have plan participants understand the options they have and to "exercise control" over their investment decisions.*

tent of Web sites include? Below are some key areas where Web site usage can be the most valuable.

- **Plan documents** should be available to all plan participants and represent a low-cost method to offer access to plan participants as an alternative to printed plan information. As discussed in Part 2, employers must strive to make plan document information accessible and understandable. While the availability of documents does not address the latter objective, it can clearly meet the prior objective if properly communicated to those who have access to the Internet at work or at home.

  Augmenting plan document information with summary plan descriptions and frequently asked questions (FAQs) can help with the latter objective of making plan information understandable.

- **Plan policies,** including investment and other operating policies that are placed on the Web site, offer the opportunity to acquaint plan participants with decision-maker aims and processes. When combined with ongoing communication, this can be a powerful educational tool. As mentioned in the previous chapter, it is important to stress that it is not enough to place policies on the Web site. Their utility for fiduciaries is best achieved when they consult them to determine action and reference to communicate action.

- **Forms and other administrative documents** in electronic format provide ready access to participants and eligible employees and can streamline transactions. As more and more employers develop systems to provide electronic interaction, this component will gain importance as a means of streamlining administrative efficiency, improving accuracy and meeting changing customer services expectations.

- **Performance standards and guarantees** should be included on the Web site both to advertise what commitment the employer and provider have made and as a means of monitoring whether commitments have been kept. Again, it will be important for the Web site to summarize performance standards and guarantees and to reference those standards when reports and measurements have been gathered and assessed.

- **General plan and investment education** is increasingly available through both the plan provider and general Web sites. This area represents a crucial opportunity for employers and providers to maximize their impact on plan participant knowledge and decision making. For those employers that are reluctant or unable to provide investment advice, this area represents the best chance to elevate participant understanding and the consequences of choices.

If investment advice is not offered, the Web site can and should include risk self-assessment tools, general asset allocation strategies and basic benchmark comparison information. Individuals who access this information should be offered some opportunity to meet with provider representatives in person or by phone to explore more detailed strategies and options along lines identified in Interpretive Bulletin 96-1 as discussed in Chapter 2.4.

Internet sites also provide an additional chance to announce upcoming group meetings, specific events, new services or options. Advertising scheduled informational sessions well in advance and referring to them in other published announcements allow employers to communicate repeatedly their programs and the importance they attach to providing access to important educational opportunities. Using Web sites over and over to communicate current and updated information increases the likelihood that plan participants will access it again and again and consider it a resource for up-to-date information.

• **Investment advice** represents the new frontier of plan services that all decision makers should understand. This component has been intentionally separated from investment education to differentiate the unique options that are available (and because there are different standards for persons providing investment advice). As mentioned earlier, education and advice are likely to come closer together over time. It will be important, though, for decision makers to understand what differentiates one from the other and to assure that both education and advice is provided within the legislative, regulatory and legal parameters that have been established (and discussed in Part 2).

While Web-based information is likely to spread into other media (for example, computer-based learning or Internet tutorials), employers will ben-

> *Increasingly, public sector employer DB plans are building sophisticated Web site capabilities for plan participants to assess their plan benefits and in so doing are building one part of the bridge that can ultimately link DB and DC assets and strategies.*

efit from understanding Web-based design and utility. Investment advice, in most settings, focuses primarily on fund options within the plan. Even if it accounts for other retirement income sources, it rarely takes advantage of the sophisticated tools or exact income amounts to refine estimates and assess retirement strategies. For example, while models may incorporate defined benefit (DB) resources on an estimated basis, they do not often differentiate between multiple DB retirement options offered by the employer nor utilize the specific or exact age-service-income formulas and calculations increasingly available from DB plans.

Remember one of Treasury's recommendations in its 96-1 Bulletin? Investment/retirement strategies are best based on the incorporation of all retirement sources (DB, spousal, Social Security and other financial resources). Increasingly, public sector employer DB plans are building sophisticated Web site capabilities for plan participants to assess their plan benefits and in so doing are building one part of the bridge that can ultimately link DB and defined contribution assets and strategies.

Funding Employer Costs

The historical inactivity in managing deferred compensation /defined contribution (DC) plans meant that employers had little cost associated with this benefit. Employers often assumed costs associated with payroll modifications, rudimentary education (especially regarding eligibility and basic plan parameters) and ongoing administration (both general and specific such as hardships, catch-up provisions and domestic relations orders). In some cases, the employer's financial support of these activities may have formed the basis for the employer accepting ongoing responsibility for costs and may have been codified in collective bargaining agreements.

As discussed in Part 2, the changing/growing responsibilities of decision makers mandate more active management of this benefit. More active management means more cost. Funding the cost to manage the DC responsibilities appropriately is a pivotal decision by employers. It could not come at a worse time. State, county, city, school district, hospital and municipality budgets are strained across the country.

> *Given the bleak financial condition of public sector employers, do they not have the ability, maybe even the right and responsibility, to avoid costs in this area when so many other public sector responsibilities face elimination or reduction? Unfortunately, and most assuredly, they do not. The granting of this financial hardship is not defensible.*

The current public sector financial shortages assure that many hard questions will confront policy-making bodies. What employer will easily decide to commit precious resources to fulfilling fiduciary responsibilities (even if they understand and accept those responsibilities)? How will the commitment of those resources withstand outside public scrutiny? To be sure, outside public constituents will review and would prefer to see employer resources, especially in financially difficult times, committed to the major public and community responsibilities that are their primary charge. If employers are forced to choose between fulfilling public commitments or complying with fiduciary responsibilities, how will policy-making bodies intelligently make their decision?

Given the bleak financial condition of public sector employers, do they not have the ability, maybe even the right and responsibility, to avoid costs in this area when so many other public sector responsibilities face elimination or reduction? Unfortunately, and most assuredly, they do not. The granting of *this* financial hardship is not defensible.

> *In a request for proposal (RFP) process, it is important first to define reasonable reimbursable expenses and then provide that total to prospective RFP respondents to assure that it is not a variable in the selection of the provider. Unless a respondent is unable to provide the requested amount, this variable should not be a factor in selection.*

How then are employers to pay for the increasing costs that legitimately arise from growing responsibilities? It is appropriate that plan expenses be paid by the plan. The determination of cost, however, is not such an easy decision to make because it is based on numerous factors and complex decisions and consequences. Purpose, type and frequency of services all influence cost. Organizational preferences and prior collective bargaining agreements may also be influential. Employers that have already begun to fund costs generally through plan assets base them on one of several approaches:

1.   As a **percentage of assets paid by the provider.** This approach yields an inconsistent result. Is it appropriate in times when assets climb to have more revenue than is necessary? Conversely, is it appropriate when assets decline to sacrifice stated objectives, services and activ-

ities because of insufficient financial support? Even if an agreement is written to permit change in the percentage based upon specified criteria, this option represents more administrative and oversight responsibility.

2. As a **percentage of assets or stated amount paid by the participant.** This option has the chief shortcoming of the first option. It also presents to each plan participant a visible, specific reminder that "additional" individual costs are being charged. It is likely that participants will compare their cost with their perceived usage of services. Also, any increases in amounts are likely to generate further participant reaction.

3. As a **stated amount paid by the provider to the plan.** This approach allows the decision makers to assess, independently of resources, what the fundamental, appropriate services and corresponding cost represent. The amount can certainly vary from one employer to another based on what type of services they choose to include, who provides and receives services (especially training for decision makers and support staff) and with what frequency services are provided. Under this approach, the provider typically provides the agreed-upon amount, usually quarterly.

4. As a **reimbursement of actual employer cost** associated with plan administration assessed to the provider or to the plan participant. Some entities, like many state plans, are required by law or ordinance to "charge back" any costs for administration of this benefit to the plan and its participants. For these entities, they have no choice except to bill participants directly although they may have some discretion in what expenses are included in the cost.

In a request for proposal (RFP) process, it is important first to define reasonable reimbursable expenses and then provide that total to prospective RFP respondents to assure that it is not a variable in the selection of the provider. For example, if the amount is not identified and various respondents propose varying amounts of reimbursement, how will decision makers assure that the amount of the reimbursement is *not* a variable in respondent selection? To avoid this problem, the determination of the amount should be made in advance of solicitation of proposals; and, unless a respondent is unable to provide the requested amount, this variable should not be a factor in selection.

It is also important to note that only costs associated with the plan can be paid with dollars received from plan participants or the provider. While it is perfectly within a fiduciary's right to bill for any and all plan costs, it would be a breach-of-fiduciary responsibility to include employer costs or add costs that do not directly inure to the benefit of plan participants. This is especially true when expenses like office space or legal support services would already have to be provided and financed by the employer. Here it is valuable to remember the discussion in Part 2 regarding the fiduciary's responsibility to limit plan expenses.

> *Employers must be certain that they fully disclose to plan participants the services they are purchasing and the corresponding plan cost of those services. This provides an excellent opportunity for employers to educate plan participants about changing decision-maker responsibilities and associated costs.*

Whatever approach is identified above, employers must be certain that they fully disclose to plan participants the services they are purchasing and the corresponding plan cost of those services. This provides an excellent opportunity for employers to educate plan participants about changing decision-maker responsibilities and associated costs.

If an employer has decided it does wish to pursue reimbursement for plan expenses, what types of expenses should it consider? Below are the general categories that employers may incorporate into their assessment and definition of reasonable reimbursable expenses:

- **Educational expenses,** whether they incorporate in-house offered programs, provider-offered programs, neutral third-party education (e.g., NAGDCA, International Foundation of Employee Benefit Plans, InFRE or International Personnel Management Association) or consultant-broker-provided programs. As mentioned above, the decision about *who* receives training is often as critical in determining overall cost as the type, amount and frequency of training that is appropriate.

- **Administrative expenses (specifically related to offering plan benefits)** including payroll, information technology and administrative personnel or support staff. This can also include costs for internally designed Web site activities, print brochures, telephone expenses, space allocation costs for offices or internal/external meetings, or mailings and postage. The decision regarding personnel and space is often a big factor in determining cost for this expense. This is also the area where past agreements, including negotiated collective bargaining agreements, may influence decisions.

- **Legal/legislative expenses (specifically related to offering plan benefits)** including internal legal support or contracted legal services (provider contracts, plan documents, Investment Policy review and modification). Any internal or external services that are used to determine what legislative or regulatory compliance is required may also be considered. In this area, it is not only legitimate but also financially prudent to utilize provider legal services as much as possible if internal resources are unavailable. While providers will legitimately and understandably qualify their assistance with the caveat that they do "not provide legal advice," the provider in-house legal staff monitor legislative, legal and regulatory changes with sufficient regularity that their assistance is often comprehensive and accurate.

- **Consulting expenses (specifically related to offering plan benefits)** can include services for competitive processes (contracting, RFPs, requests for disclosure), assistance with policy development (investment, fiduciary, education or communication policies) educational training, fund performance review and/or administrative services review.

> *Employers that choose not to obtain expenses from the plan face one of two distinctly problematic choices. They must fund costs from the employer when employer resources may be scarce. They must minimize or eliminate activities that jeopardize their ability to meet fiduciary and due diligence requirements.*

Employers that choose not to obtain expenses from the plan face one of two distinctly problematic choices. They must fund costs from the employer when employer resources may be scarce. They must minimize or eliminate activities that jeopardize their ability to meet fiduciary and due diligence requirements.

PART 4

Participant Education

> *"The educated differ from the uneducated as much as the living do from the dead."*
>
> *Aristotle*

The Education Challenge

This section should begin with an acknowledgment. Irrespective of where the deferred compensation/defined contribution (DC) function is located (benefits, human resources, finance, retirement), the increased responsibility discussed throughout this book represents additional work for individuals who are already amply occupied with myriad other responsibilities. This is one more on top of many.

Nevertheless, the strategies and resources employers commit to this responsibility can directly benefit participants and avoid or minimize liability. Handled properly, they can be efficient and effective in meeting employer and employee needs.

This book began with a quote from Shakespeare's *Tempest*. It described the term *sea change*. As the passage visually illustrates, a sea change represents a total transformation from one form to another. Bones into coral. Eyes into pearls. The sea change that is reshaping deferred compensation/DC management is not in the creation of plan documents or the communication of greater portability and maximum contributions. As fundamentally important as they are, it is not even the reconfiguration of how decision makers make decisions. The sea change is in the education of plan participants.

Education is currently being provided, to be sure. In fact, critical legislative and regulatory changes have prompted more education today than has probably ever taken place before. It is not enough. It is not nearly enough.

At its very heart, the *raison d'etre* of deferred compensation is individual retirement savings. The very breath of DC is education.

> *This book began with a quote from*
> *Shakespeare's* **Tempest.** *It described the term* **sea change.**
> *As the passage visually illustrates, a sea change*
> *represents a total transformation from one form*
> *to another. Bones into coral. Eyes into pearls.*
> *The sea change that is reshaping deferred*
> *compensation/DC management is not in the*
> *creation of plan documents or the communication*
> *of greater portability and maximum contributions.*
> *As fundamentally important as it is, it is not*
> *even the reconfiguration of how decision makers*
> *make decisions. The sea change is in the*
> *education of plan participants.*

All employers could benefit from assessing their and their provider's strategies and actions. They might benefit by quizzing themselves with the following Education Challenge: Self-Assessment Tool, and grading their results. The self-assessment checklist printed on the following pages has been duplicated in Part 5 as a sample document for the convenience of readers who want to copy and use it. It comes with the invitation that it be shared with other provider representatives or employer decision makers to see the composite score of the overall assessment.

The authors would be bold enough to assert that even those employers with the highest marks will come away from the challenge understanding exactly how haphazard their educational programs are and what additional steps they might consider taking.

With education, young employees **understand** the value of making contributions early and using the length of their career to amass sufficient resources for their retirement. They know that it is never too early to start and that the early contributions, even if small, produce greater results than larger contributions later. In a perhaps more poetic way, they avoid the chief shortcoming so eloquently voiced by Oscar Wilde in his *Picture of Dorian Grey*, "To get back one's youth, one has merely to repeat one's follies."

Do employers:

☐ Communicate to young employees how vital early contributions are?

☐ Target young employees with educational material that substantiates the enormous value of early contributions?

☐ Offer regular training to demonstrate these values?

☐ Use incentives to increase young employee participation?

☐ Monitor the number of participants by age?

☐ Assess where communication and education efforts might be most successful?

With education, participants **understand** that they must know themselves and their financial needs and objectives for investment strategies to work. They must know how tolerant they are of risk. They must have a general idea of when they plan to retire, and they must have some rudimentary sense of what they think they need to retire on satisfactorily and successfully. Perhaps most importantly, they must be able to correlate their knowledge with broad-based factual information regarding retirement trends and population-based information to assure that their individual expectations are in line with established characteristics.

Do employers:

☐ Utilize self-assessment tools that allow participants to determine their risk tolerance, retirement objectives and time horizon?

☐ Make these tools accessible and provide guidance on how participants may use the tools to evaluate their individual needs and preferences?

☐ Identify methods to promote their use by all plan participants?

☐ Measure the success of their efforts?

With education, participants **understand** that the strategies to build their retirement savings can change or evolve during their life and that such change and evolution requires that they revisit their objectives and strategies regularly. They use these self-assessments to rebalance their portfolios and adjust their overall retirement objectives and expectations.

Do employers:

☐ Develop training programs that identify how investment strategies may change over the career of an individual based on marriage, birth, divorce and other family status changes?

☐ Target life cycle training to individuals to capture the changing needs of participants at different times in their careers?

☐ Measure the ways in which individuals should modify their investments as they age and approach retirement?

With education, participants **understand** that their selection of investments and the allocation of contributions to each investment type is the optimal way to achieve their retirement objectives. They know that pursuing "hot investments" and the "fund du jour" will thwart their aims. They know that the opposite strategy of investing in fixed account or stable value funds throughout their career will lead to an ongoing erosion of retirement assets. Somehow, they must understand and overcome the inherent disadvantage in Mark Twain's spurious advice: "October. This is one of the peculiarly dangerous months to speculate in stocks. The others are July, January, September, April, November, May, March, June, December, August and February."

Do employers:

☐ Unshackle participants of the notion that their success is not improved by pursuing a particular fund or fund category but by having participants understand the value of asset allocation over fund selection?

☐ Demonstrate their confidence in replacing underperforming funds, however popular, with the knowledge that their participants understand and accept the change?

☐ Develop programs to educate participants about the historical failure of individuals who "time the market" or follow hot funds?

> *The sea change in education will result in precisely these kinds of understandings by plan participants. Those employers that think they already have robust and successful educational programs have only to survey their plan participants to know they have failed the educational litmus test. Those providers who think they offer the most stellar, competitive educational programs have only to look at the participation rates, the allocation percentages (individually and in the aggregate), and the general knowledge of their plan participants to know that such claims are empty.*

With education, participants **understand** that a proper evaluation of retirement resources must include all resources, their own and their spouses', to be thoughtfully balanced. They expect to include in any self-assessment the DC sources as well as employer defined benefit (DB) plan payments, Social Security income, other outside resources and, where appropriate, spousal resources.

Do employers:

☐ Structure their self-assessment programs to allow employees to incorporate all sources of retirement income?

☐ Provide guidance to employees in how to structure portfolios based on the total sources of potential retirement income?

☐ Use tools that allow participants to incorporate outside assets in their portfolio assumptions and wealth accumulation projections?

☐ Collaborate with internal DB providers to coordinate DB/DC resources into a single model that participants can understand and easily use?

☐ Establish specific expectations as to how these tools will be promoted to assure maximum use?

With education, participants **understand** that changes in career are not opportunities to liberate funds for immediate purposes, however compelling the purpose, even, for instance, the purchase of a home. They know a commitment to retirement requires a disciplined commitment to contributing and an equally disciplined commitment to maintaining assets intact for retirement.

Do employers:

- ☐ Develop programs to provide exiting employees with information regarding the importance of retaining their retirement assets?

- ☐ Discuss with incoming employees the value of transferring into employer programs existing assets that are located elsewhere?

- ☐ Assure that terminated employees receive the same information and educational opportunities that active and retired employee participants enjoy.

With education, lower salaried employees, especially single parent employees, **understand** that their circumstances are not a prohibition to participate but a challenge. It's a challenge that can be overcome using the knowledge they can gain regarding financial resource management and tax advantages. Women, in particular, recognize that precisely because they have traditionally lower salaries than men and longer life expectancies after retirement, these contributions are more critical for retirement security.

Do employers:

- ☐ Target outreach efforts to lower salaried workers and customize programs to acknowledge the greater difficulty and importance of these individuals contributing to a DC program?

- ☐ Focus on tax advantages for lower income participants?

- ☐ Integrate DC contributions in the larger context of overall financial planning strategies for these individuals?

With education, participants **understand** that their proximity to retirement requires special review and consideration. They need to be aware that longer life spans may require ongoing long-term commitment and not massive overhaul of investment strategy.

Do employers:

- ☐ Incorporate DC objectives in financial planning and preretirement seminars to highlight the value of catch-up provisions, rebalancing, reassessing retirement objectives?

- ☐ Meet with retirees or preretirees on a regular basis?

- ☐ Incorporate information about life expectancy and the impact on retirement assets?

With education, retirees **understand** that they are unlikely to find competitive offers, in either investment support or general education, through individual brokers or companies, however tempting and however familiar and friendly their relationships with individual brokers. They recognize that these companies and their employees are investing substantial amounts in marketing campaigns to attract individual, high-asset participants and that this marketing barrage does not mean that they provide a superior investment or better services.

Do employers:

- ☐ Assess the number of retirees and the amount of assets being "lost" from employer plans as a result of migration to individual brokers?

- ☐ Offer information or education regarding rollover considerations to counteract the significant marketing campaign undertaken by companies in the wake of the new portability afforded as a result of the Economic Growth and Tax Relief Reconciliation Act (EGTRRA)?

- ☐ Provide retirees with the tools to evaluate both the advantages and disadvantages of transferring funds to individual retirement accounts?

- ☐ Offer counseling programs in recognition that retirees are still customers and still deserve the continued educational services to help them make informed decisions throughout their retirement years?

The sea change in education will result in precisely these kinds of understandings by plan participants. Those employers that think they already have robust and successful educational programs have only to survey their plan participants to know they have failed the educational litmus test. Those providers who think they offer the most stellar, competitive educational programs have only to look at the participation rates, the allocation percentages (individually and in the aggregate) and the general knowledge of their plan participants to know that such claims are empty. There is much more that needs to be done.

The examination of public sector investor patterns would make anyone wonder whether public sector plan participants had fully subscribed to Mark Twain's vision of investment strategy: "There are two times in a man's life when he shouldn't speculate: when he can't afford it, and when he can."

> *So, if everyone is doing such a miserable job educating plan participants, what actions can and should be taken to meet the above challenges more successfully?*
> *It starts, like every journey, with a clear understanding about where you want to go, how you plan to get there and what commitment it will require.*

The purpose of the above challenge and commentary on educational plans is not to berate employers and providers for shabby efforts to educate plan participants. It is certainly not to suggest that their aims are spurious or their concerns heartless. In short, it is not an indictment. It is intended, however, as a challenge, to say that the way ahead stretches out so much farther than the way behind and that smug satisfaction with current efforts unfolds like pride before the fall. Employers and providers must devote more resources and strategies to deferred compensation/DC plan participant education because education is the foundation for long-term, intelligent investing.

The migration of employer-sponsored retirement plans from DB plans to DC plans demands that we roll up our sleeves and tackle the problem of rampant participant misunderstanding. The re-emergence of market volatility after unprecedented market growth demands that we reacquaint participants with tried and true principles of investing. Promoting understanding that retirement asset growth is neither a right nor a predetermined outcome of conservative investment strategies but a balanced, long-term commitment to an informed, self-identified purpose of retirement asset building should be a standard goal of employers and providers alike. Retirement asset growth is not a manifest destiny.

So, if everyone is doing such a miserable job educating plan participants, what actions can and should be taken to meet the above challenges more successfully? It starts, like every journey, with a clear understanding about where you want to go, how you plan to get there and what commitment it will require.

> *The re-emergence of market volatility after unprecedented market growth demands that we reacquaint participants with (the) understanding that retirement asset growth is neither a right nor a predetermined outcome of conservative investment strategies but a balanced, long-term commitment to an informed, self-identified purpose of retirement asset building. Retirement asset growth is not a manifest destiny.*

It also begins with an understanding that you never really arrive. You are never done. There is always room for improvement. In ancient Greece, Plato described two worlds, the "world of being" and the "world of becoming." No one lived in the world of being. It was ethereal and unreachable. Instead, everyone inhabited the world of becoming. Did that make the world of being irrelevant or unimportant? Quite the contrary. The world of being was and is the model. The way ahead. The world of becoming is the unending quest to emulate the model. It is never finished. Prospective legislation, evolutionary educational tools, employee turnover and the general volatility of benefits in general assure employers that the educational task is never complete.

Defining Educational Objectives

Employers that made a sincere effort to answer the questions on the preceding Education Challenge: Self-Assessment Tool have the basic ingredients for developing their educational objectives. For those that had neither the time nor inclination to respond to such a checklist, it is critical to understand that the most efficient and effective means of delivering education is to be clear about defining its purpose. In order to define that purpose, there must be some sense of what is important, what works and how resources can be focused.

> *Educated participants invest more and are likely to invest more wisely. Increased participation, increased contributions and larger per capita assets are objectives that both the employer and provider can easily embrace.*

Comprehensive education requires clarity about its usefulness. Any course of study demands identifiable proficiency at the end. When we think of undergraduate or graduate education, we think of a prescribed course of study that leads to a degree, a symbol that an individual has attained a certain level of knowledge and the ability to use that knowledge. It is helpful to apply this same model to retirement planning and education. Education on retirement strategies generally and deferred compensation/defined contribution (DC) plans specifically profits from a comprehensive approach to building knowledge.

After all, educated participants invest more and are likely to invest more wisely. Wiser investment is likely to result in greater investment growth. Increased participation, increased contributions and larger-per-capita assets are objectives that both the employer and provider can easily embrace.

Questions are the cornerstone of any good strategy. The questions an organization asks itself of its policies, procedures, processes and aims are often more revealing than the answers because questions denote strategy. Answers may result from strategy but they could just as easily arise from indifference, apathy or thoughtless reaction.

An engineer knows before the building begins what the structure will look like when it is finished and what foundation is necessary to support its structure. Who would contemplate creating a foundation without having a clear concept of what the ultimate structure will be? An organization must be no less clear about what it is building and what its "building" will look like when it is completed. All that clarity occurs before it pours the concrete or lays the first brick.

In order to begin building the foundation for participant education, the following are some of the questions that employers should explore. What's the educational "degree" you want participants to have at the end? If you have an ideal deferred compensation participant, what will he or she know? How will the participant use information to develop tactics to achieve his or her own retirement objectives? What information should the participant seek? In what form or medium should the participant prefer to get it? In what order will it be provided or received? How will we measure whether it is received and understood? These are important questions to ask. The answers by any organization determine both the structure and the foundation.

The answers to these types of questions and the definition of educational purpose for plan participants constitutes, for lack of better words, an employer Education Policy.

Chapter 3.6 discussed the Education Policy as it covers decision-maker responsibilities and objectives. This section covers the policy from the perspective of participant education. Decision makers can adopt two education policies, one for fiduciaries, one for participants; or they can combine both into a single policy that covers all the plan's educational objectives.

The content of an Education Policy for participants is essentially organized along the lines of the questions asked in the previous chapter. As a result, the core of any Participant Education Policy should include the following:

- **Overall purpose.** The employer should clearly articulate the basic objectives or purpose of the Education Policy. Is it to have all participants, potential participants and retirees know enough to make truly informed, self-interested investment decisions? Is it to have these individuals know the basic characteristics of funds and how those funds are evaluated on a plan and individual level? Is it to have participants reassess their investment strategies and objectives at appropriate intervals?

It is also helpful, in the Purpose Statement, to identify who the recipients of education are. They should certainly include active participants but the omission of retirees or employee nonparticipants would be inappropriately myopic. An important question for employers to answer is: Are there stakeholders other than participants, retirees and employee nonparticipants that should be included? If they remain part of the plan, should terminated employees be considered? If the employer wishes to accentuate its difference in DC support and guidance as a means of enhancing its recruitment efforts, are prospective employees important to consider? What about spouses and other family members?

It may be helpful to review the critical components of Interpretive Bulletin 96-1 in determining overall purpose. Remember the initial recommendation: "Individual participants and beneficiaries should consider their other assets, income and investments (outside the plan) when applying an asset allocation model or using interactive investment material." The greatest shortcoming of contemporary asset allocation models is their implicit assumption that they are the entirety of retirement assets. Do asset allocation models become more effective when they incorporate/consider other asset sources?

Remember too, the Department of Labor explained, to furnish "general financial and investment information on estimating future retirement income needs, determining investment time horizons and assessing risk tolerance" linked to specific investments so plan participants could "relate basic retirement planning concepts to their individual situations." What then, is the role of investment advice compared to investment education? Remember the continuum of education and advice? What elements on that continuum are important to provide? How far to the right on the continuum (toward advice) is the employer willing to go?

- **Key roles/responsibilities.** Whether part of the purpose section or in a separate section, it is valuable to specify what roles and responsibilities each stakeholder has. This provides an opportunity for the employers to summarize the new roles and responsibilities they have and the ways their changing roles and responsibilities have impacted their management of this benefit. It is helpful, as an example, for employers to communicate that they must review funds periodically and that underperforming funds must be removed and replaced with better performing funds. That is really no longer an option. It is a requirement. There is value in having the participants understand that requirement. Explaining the processes by which actions are taken and the criteria upon which decisions are based is no less important.

What, though, are the responsibilities of other stakeholders? What roles do providers play in education? How are their processes and decisions made? If consultants or actuaries are used, what roles and responsibilities do they have?

> *If there is one stakeholder group that is conspicuously omitted from the list of roles and responsibilities, it is clearly the participants. How many employers articulate the responsibilities plan participants have?*

If there is one stakeholder group that is conspicuously omitted from the list of roles and responsibilities, it is clearly the participants. How many employers articulate the responsibilities plan participants have? Do they have a responsibility to learn about their own objectives and preferences and to apply them to their investment strategies? Should they be aware of plan parameters and fundamental guidelines? Should they be aware of differences in investment types and the ways different investments are monitored? If ultimately, participants make self-interested investment selections, how is that self-interest determined? Do they have the responsibility to rethink their investments when their own individual circumstances change? If, by their very nature, DC plans are participant-directed, is it not reasonable to expect the participant to learn sufficient information to direct investments in a self-interested way?

The answers to these and other similar questions about participant roles and responsibilities will help both the employer and provider design educational programs that facilitate participant development in areas where the participant needs to gain greater awareness and needs to use that awareness in his or her own decision-making responsibilities.

It is so critical to remember, that participants in a self-directed DC plan fundamentally differ from participants in a DB plan. Why?

Because in the former they have a role; they have a responsibility. That role and responsibility do not exist in the latter. If they have a responsibility, what is it? Shouldn't it be clearly defined and communicated to individuals? And what responsibility does the employer have to distinguish the participant's responsibility from that of the employer, the provider and the fiduciaries?

This role does not imply that plan participants must or would be willing to expend the time required of undergraduates or graduates to earn a "degree." Nor does it suggest that participants are likely to undertake the same disciplined approach that DB fiduciaries take in fund selection and monitoring.

Admittedly, many plan participants have neither the time nor the interest in becoming an informed investor. Their needs are much simpler, much more basic. They want to invest money. In most cases, they want someone else to guide them with their investments and that represents the extent of the commitment they wish to make. It is for these individuals that the growth of investment advice services is most beneficial.

> *Precisely because investors run the gamut from disinterested and unwilling to commit time, to sophisticated, knowledgeable and willing to commit time that employers benefit from clearly expressing the roles and responsibilities of participants and recognizing that those roles will vary depending on the investor.*

Precisely because investors run the gamut from disinterested and unwilling to commit time, to sophisticated, knowledgeable and willing to commit time that employers benefit from clearly expressing the roles and responsibilities of participants and recognizing that those roles will vary depending on the investor. Of equal importance, the education and the mode of disseminating the education must also vary to meet the needs of the diverse investor population.

There is enormous value in investing the time to raise these questions and conscientiously answering them. There is enormous value in communicating them to plan participants so that all stakeholders understand both their and their employer's role and responsibilities.

• **Educational organization/content.** Plan participants benefit from being able to see the organizational structure of the education platform the employer has adopted. What undergraduate or graduate student would contemplate a professional degree in any area without wanting to see the complete courses that must be taken to complete a degree? By seeing the entire organizational structure of education, plan participants can observe quickly both the employer/provider thoughtfulness that went into its organization and the areas where further information is necessary or helpful to aid in their fund selection.

Remember the story about the blind men in the room with the elephant? Each blind man touches a different part of the animal and draws conclusions about what it is. Plan participants are left similarly blind if they are not presented with the whole. They are unable to see where their greatest educational/informational growth area is. In short, they are hamstrung by not being able to prioritize the information that will be most helpful to their individual efforts.

As will be seen in the next several chapters, the authors recommend a comprehensive "course of study" that progressively provides increasingly sophisticated information to elevate the participants' understanding of tools and methodologies in their efforts to maximize retirement assets. Readers can adopt the recommended structure or elect a different organization. It is important to emphasize that it is not the specifics of the structure but the employer identification of what constitutes the entirety of education that is most critical.

- **Information medium/access.** Because technology provides increasing options for how information is provided, it is important to consider what medium is most efficient and effective in educating plan participants. Most employers are likely to find that a buffet is best. Let participants pick and choose what works best for them.

What information and education is available on the Internet? Is there a place for self-paced computer-based learning that allows participants to gain knowledge at their own convenience and pace? If so, how is this best communicated? What informational/educational resources are best delivered and accessed through face-to-face meetings on an individual or group basis? What should be reserved for print medium?

Is some information better delivered from one messenger rather than another? Earlier, we emphasized that neither labor nor management can represent labor or management in the decision-making processes. That is not to say that they would not have inherently greater effectiveness in reaching plan participants with particular messages. If that assumption is true, what information should come from the employer? What might best come from labor? What should be left to providers? How should messages be coordinated?

The assessment and communication to participants of how the employer and provider use media to provide information and education provides an important, comprehensive guide to plan participants on how they may access information efficiently depending on their preferences.

Access and media also drive frequency of educational efforts. How frequently are group meetings held? How frequently are provider representatives available to plan participants? How often are Internet, print or other communication efforts announced or marketed?

> *No educational institution could hope to be attractive or successful if it were unable to clearly state what classes lead to what degrees. DC educational efforts that are launched without consideration of purpose, roles and responsibilities, organizational structure and assessment of appropriate media will perpetuate haphazard efforts and dubious outcomes. If neither the employer nor the provider can be clear about these fundamental prerequisites of education, they can neither pretend nor hope that plan participants will be better informed.*

No educational institution could hope to be attractive or successful if it were unable to clearly state what classes lead to what degrees. DC educational efforts that are launched without consideration of purpose, roles and responsibilities, organizational structure and assessment of appropriate media will perpetuate haphazard efforts and dubious outcomes. If neither the employer nor the provider can be clear about these fundamental prerequisites of education, they can neither pretend nor hope that plan participants will be better informed. They cannot hope to have participants earn a "degree" and graduate.

Phase of Life Education

We have compared participant education to an academic institution education throughout Part 4. Perhaps an explanation is overdue. An academic education is a well-thought-out course of study, a progression of knowledge that leads to some end. Admittedly, the correlation ignores the practical limitations that exist for the vast majority of plan participants. Very few individuals can or will commit significant time to this endeavor. Participants have other legitimate priorities that make the comparison less than perfect.

We have chosen to compare academic study to participant education for two main reasons. First, as with the academic institution's organization of freshman to senior years, participant education can intelligently be divided into four main categories: (1) entry level, young employee, (2) midcareer, (3) preretirement and (4) retirement.

Second, the progression of study allows individuals to progress along a continuum that increases their familiarity with and understanding of the optimal way to invest.

There is nothing particularly sacrosanct about this comparison. The use of a four-year education model for designing defined contribution (DC) programs is a paradigm. But the value of the paradigm is the utility of its organizational structure. Students come to college with different skill sets and knowledge. So do plan participants. Students have a wide variety of interests and aims. So do plan participants. Students may change courses and fields of study multiple times. Participants often need to adjust their strategies regularly to reflect changes in their lives. Students who are clear about the courses they must take to earn a degree are more efficient and effective in completing that degree within an "appropriate" time. Investors who understand the knowledge they must have to meet their own retirement objectives are likely to accumulate wealth more successfully.

The value of the comparison is that the path to an academic degree and the path to a self-interested investment lie through a progression of educational growth.

In the case of DC plans, that growth starts as a new employee continues through the midterm of one's professional career, incorporates the planned transition from career to retirement and concludes with sound retirement investment and distribution during the retirement years.

It is appropriate to discuss asset allocation models briefly before discussing the broader application of various asset classes to investment strategies and the way these strategies influence investment selection at various ages.

Since the inception of general securities, the best long-term historical performance has been in equities. Many participants in DC plans, unfortunately, were invested in stable value or fixed interest accounts during the 1990s. As a result, they failed to take advantage of the significant gains in equity funds throughout that period. Conversely, many investors in this same market period were heavily invested in equities and failed to act as the equity market began a slide into a 36-month bear market, therefore losing a significant portion of their investment value. Both groups were guilty of not adhering to a basic tenet of investing, namely, diversification.

Asset allocation funds (or model portfolios) were established as a direct response to the need for participants (who often do not have the time to configure their own portfolio) who recognize that: (1) diversification is important, (2) adverse impact may be avoided or lessened by diversification and (3) placement of all funds in fixed or stable value accounts may be eroded by inflationary changes or taxation at distribution.

Asset allocation fund models vary significantly. The most basic models, and those that are most extensively used in the public sector, offer between three and five fund categories ranging from conservative to aggressive. Figure 5 represents a fairly common five-fund model portfolio for asset allocation funds.

As most asset allocation fund designs are currently applied, they anticipate single investors or individuals whose primary retirement vehicle is in DC plans. Are they as appropriate for public sector DC plans, especially if defined benefit (DB) plans are also present? Sadly, asset allocation models are designed to work more effectively for private sector plans than their public sector counterparts precisely because they often ignore the impact the participant's DB plan has on overall portion of assets to be allocated.

Those public sector employers that offer a DB plan provide a significant retirement funding source for long-term employees. DB retirement formulas range from 2% to 3% per year at ages ranging from 50 to 65 years old with service levels generally of 20 to 30 years.

Figure 5

ASSET ALLOCATION FUND MODEL

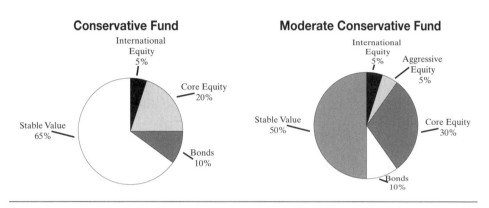

Conservative Fund

International Equity 5%
Core Equity 20%
Stable Value 65%
Bonds 10%

Moderate Conservative Fund

International Equity 5%
Aggressive Equity 5%
Stable Value 50%
Core Equity 30%
Bonds 10%

Moderate Fund

International Equity 10%
Aggressive Equity 10%
Stable Value 30%
Core Equity 40%
Bonds 10%

Moderate Aggressive Fund

International Equity 15%
Bonds 20%
Aggressive Equity 15%
Core Equity 50%

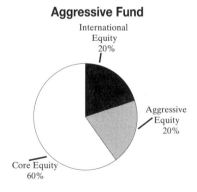

Aggressive Fund

International Equity 20%
Aggressive Equity 20%
Core Equity 60%

While these formulas can be confusing, in simple language, the retirement monthly check may range from 50% to 100% of preretirement earnings. This monthly continuation of income coupled with an anticipated reduction of expenses at retirement provides a comfortable cushion for many long-term employed retirees. For those plans that offer cost of living adjustments (CO-LAs), the impact of inflation (which is a significant issue in DC plans) may be largely mitigated. Social Security or spousal income further enhances retirement resources.

Where DB plans are in place, is the historical asset allocation model appropriate? If so, shouldn't the DB plan represent the conservative portion of this investment model or be factored into the available assets before investment selections are made? It certainly should.

Despite the importance of accounting for all assets (and certainly assets as significant as those in most DB plans), there is no public sector customized asset allocation model that incorporates or accounts for DB plan assets and potential retiree payments. A more appropriate public sector asset allocation model might best be modified to reflect the conservative stable value and bond holdings and emphasize the variable components and associated risk.

Providers have not considered the ways in which asset allocation models might be redesigned to provide a more balanced allocation in public sector environments. Nor have they evaluated the role asset allocation models might represent as an alternative to the current preponderance of public sector participant investment in stable value or fixed funds.

The reasons for provider inactivity in this area are understandable even if unpleasant. Providers have little incentive to redirect participant funds from stable value/fixed interest accounts as these options generally provide the largest profit margins of any investments offered in a provider's fund portfolio. If participants are encouraged to move *en masse* from these investments, will the provider need to rethink pricing in order to retain profitability? Almost certainly.

Asset allocation models also represent a corresponding complexity for employers because they offer little comparative source of evaluation. How are employers expected to compare one model against another? What is the appropriate benchmark? While it is true that benchmarks are identified in the prospectus, the periodic reallocation of assets makes the stated benchmarks nearly irrelevant.

How then may employers and providers identify an appropriate benchmark to evaluate their performance? Since balanced funds were the premodel for asset allocation funds, the simple answer would be to review asset allocation funds in comparison with balanced funds.

Employers and providers may consider another option. As has been discussed, DC plans offer a broad set of core investments from which participants select. Where investment policies have been implemented, plan decision makers follow their Investment Policies to evaluate the performance of these various investments. Asset allocation model design in the public sector could incorporate the exact investments available in the plan. Thusly designed, any analysis of the core investments would automatically incorporate the due diligence to the asset allocation models. If, for example, underperforming funds were replaced, the asset allocation model would automatically be reconfigured and due diligence observed.

Public sector asset allocation model design and evaluation will continue to be part of the broader issue of providing sound education to plan participants. With this discussion of general investment strategies and asset allocation models in mind, let's look at the educational components of each phase.

NEW EMPLOYEES

New employees need basic information and a fundamental understanding of basic resources and how they can access those resources. So a "freshman" curriculum may consist of:

- **Basic investment strategies.** These include pretax contributions, untaxed asset growth, basic retirement objectives, self-risk assessment, identification of retirement objectives and basic diversification.

- **Awareness of specific deferred compensation/DC plan requirements.** Because deferred compensation and DC plans are increasingly subject to similar requirements (legal/legislative parameters, maximum contribution limits, catch-up provisions, portability), providers can design education programs for an increasingly broadening group of employers and participants. Key differences, however, require customization. Nonqualified plans are still different from qualified plans: portability is different based on the types of funds that are being transferred and employers may have selected different trust vehicles for 457 plans (trust, custodian, annuity), to name a few of the distinctions.

- **Summary of employer specific documents/policies.** It is critical to familiarize new employees/plan participants with *access* to formal plan documents, investment policies, transaction forms and specialized documents (e.g., hardship withdrawal, catch-up, domestic relations orders, transfer parameters). It is unreasonable to expect that participants will in fact read the array of material and information at their disposal, but it is very reasonable to expect that they know where it is located and how they can access it for any immediate use they have.

• **Summary of employer procedures/processes.** Letting employees know how they can enroll, change contributions, access individual account information, evaluate and re-evaluate investment strategies, and account for life changes is critical.

CURRENT PARTICIPANTS

Individuals who are aware of fundamental plan characteristics and requirements are prepared for more detailed information. It is important to stress that individuals in this group represent an enormous spectrum in both their understanding and sophistication as well as their employment tenure and age. Understanding the diverse breadth of educational needs in this group is an indispensable prerequisite to success in communicating with them and having them take advantage of the information that may advance their sophistication. Curriculum in this area may include:

• **Self-assessment of risk.** Increasingly, software models allow participants to assess their own tolerance for risk based on their retirement objectives. Completing a self-assessment questionnaire (and knowing when it is appropriate to reassess tolerance for risk) is a critical first step in identifying funds and allocation.

• **Understanding risk.** Apart from individual self-assessment of risk, there is underlying risk associated with various investments. Understanding specific investment risk associated with each asset class permits participants to align their individual risk tolerance with the risk characteristics associated with individual funds.

• **Increasing knowledge of investment terminology/concepts.** Although Morningstar is clearly paving the way for providing simple, understandable ways to learn about different investment measurement tools, numerous Internet resources are available to provide simple, straightforward explanations of how investments are categorized, how they are compared to their benchmarks, what criteria are used to evaluate all funds in a particular investment category and how each tool works.

   The next generation of these tools will make it unnecessary for individuals to understand how the underlying evaluative tools assess fund performance. They will know instead the bottom-line conclusions. Irrespective of whether it is a positive evolution for participants to know little more than "five stars is good" and "one star is not good," many more complex evaluative tools will have similar, simple symbols for use.

> *It is important to stress that individuals in this group (current participants) represent an enormous spectrum in both their understanding and sophistication as well as their employment tenure and age. Understanding the diverse breadth of educational needs in this group is an indispensable prerequisite to success.*

- **Defining retirement objectives.** As simple as it may appear, many plan participants do not understand retirement objectives and asset needs. Many Americans are still woefully ill-informed of what retirement assets are necessary for the longer life and additional responsibilities (especially in health care and long-term care affordability) that face them as retirees. The news media is replete with stories about individuals who believe that the $50,000 or $100,000 they have will be sufficient to last them from retirement in their 60s to death.

  The gap between reality and belief is so vast that multiple presidential administrations have devoted significant resources through the National Summit on Retirement Savings to identifying ways in which individuals of different ages and cultural backgrounds can understand what their needs are likely to be and what resources will be required to meet those needs. While this gap is narrowed in circumstances where individuals have a sufficient DB allowance, the understanding of changing retirement needs and resources is beneficial to all groups.

- **Asset allocation funds.** Asset allocation funds or options represent a significant improvement for plan participants but they are not a panacea. Asset allocation options still require that the participants conduct a self-inventory to determine their risk tolerance, retirement objective and time horizon. It is also critical that individuals understand the internal characteristics of these types of pooled portfolios. Reassessing strategies and rebalancing based on those reassessments are no less critical.

  These types of models also represent greater difficulty for both the plan participant and the fiduciary decision maker to evaluate "net return" because the underlying performance of the diverse funds and the costs are more difficult to assess and nearly impossible to compare with other benchmarks.

Employers can augment internal DC educational programs with information about DB programs (where appropriate) and general financial/estate planning education.

PRERETIREES

While it varies from occupation to occupation and employer to employer, plan participants at some time in the years prior to retirement benefit from more focused education about how contributions and financial planning will impact final assets at retirement. Curriculum in this area may include:

- **Maximizing contributions.** Employer and providers alike fully understand the sad characteristic of young employees neither understanding nor using the power of contributions early in their careers. As employees age, their income earnings rise and their "disposable income" grows. They are capable of investing more and good education can often prompt them to invest more.

> *What is little discussed is the way the investment dynamics for this group (young employees) of individuals is changing. Because of increased earning power and longer lifespans, employees in midcareer may be able to make investments that they will not need to tap for decades to come.*

What is little discussed is the way the investment dynamics for this group (young employees) of individuals is changing. Because of increased earning power and longer life spans, employees in midcareer may be able to make investments that they will not need to tap for decades to come.

An individual who increases his or her contributions in his or her 40s, even 50s, may have 20 or more years before there is a need to utilize those resources. Having individuals understand this dynamic and the way it shapes their investment strategies because of elongated time horizons empowers them to structure their contribution levels and investment choices more appropriately.

- **Catch-up provisions.** The expansion of public sector catch-up provisions represents one of several areas where recent legislation has made

457 plans superior to their private sector qualified counterparts. Not only has the "traditional" catch-up provision been expanded to allow deferrals up to twice the annual contribution maximum (now that it is fully indexed and expanding), but the addition of age 50-plus catch-up and "deemed" or "side-car" IRAs (where they are offered) have made significant changes to the amount of money individuals can set aside on a tax-deferred basis for retirement.

While this advantage is used predominantly by upper income individuals, it is not out of the reach of midincome employees *with proper planning.* Having plan participants understand this option and its powerful benefits well in advance of their eligibility for catch-up provides them with sufficient time to amass the resources they will need to maximize value.

- **Understanding distribution options.** While distribution options may be years away during this phase, it is instructive for participants to know the expanded options that are now available to them and how their selection impacts their overall retirement planning. Individuals who elect to delay distribution entirely have different needs than those who begin systematic distributions at retirement. How their decisions impact their income and longevity of assets is an important variable in their planning.

There are special changes with this group or phase of life because there is a growing concern that millions of Americans are not prepared for, or even aware of, what is needed for a successful retirement. Baby boomers are approaching this time in their life much differently from the generation before them; and issues such as phased retirement, health care costs, solvency of the Social Security system and the possible responsibility of financial and emotional caring for aging parents are making an assessment of future retirement needs more challenging than ever before.

Studies have been conducted that explore the financial aspects of what individuals should accumulate to support themselves during these years. However, to identify the true state of retirement readiness, there needs to be a broader examination that looks at the entire retirement picture including the financial, emotional and physical risks as well as the many variable decisions that must be considered when preparing for this life phase.

The International Foundation for Retirement Education (InFRE), a non-profit foundation established in 1997, has initiated a project to begin this in-depth examination of retirement readiness. This initiative will establish a comprehensive definition of what it means to be ready for retirement at different life stages and a corresponding benchmark index that will help determine how well prepared individuals really are. The first phase of this project is being conducted by examining the retirement readiness of the federal government workforce through a contract with the Office of Personnel Management. Funding is currently being sought to conduct a broader examination of the American private and public sector employee population at-large.

RETIREES

As mentioned previously, retirees have been the forgotten stakeholders in employer and provider strategies. The Economic Growth and Tax Relief Reconciliation Act of 2001 (EGTRRA) changed all that in fact, if not in reality. It is still not apparent in employer and provider behavior that this group constitutes a critical component of overall assets and service needs.

> *The battle for retiree assets (skirmishes is perhaps a better description) is still in its early stages but few employers or providers have even acknowledged the confrontation, much less the attrition of their own resources.*

What employers and providers have misunderstood, the individual broker community has grasped all too clearly. The battle for retiree assets (skirmishes is perhaps a better description) is still in its early stages but few employers or providers have even acknowledged the confrontation, much less the attrition of their own resources.

In a head-to-head comparison, few individual brokers or brokerage houses should be able to compete with employer providers. The economies of scale clearly favor the latter. Nevertheless, retiree savings, often in sizable amounts, are being siphoned away every day. Oftentimes, sadly, the reason relates to personal connections, not optimal self-interest. At some point, however, providers will fully recognize the tactics and take measures to minimize the defections.

But retirees present special challenges for employers and providers alike. They are often geographically removed from the employers' workplaces and therefore cannot be fully integrated with on-site active employee individual and group sessions. Although retiree aversion to Internet resources is changing, retirees' accessibility to provider information and provider accessibility to them represents a difficult and arduous undertaking.

The historical foundation has been less prepared for this stakeholder group. Who would have anticipated this change in flexibility? The value of providing education to retirees prior to EGTRRA was arguably less critical. Participants could make only one or (after the Small Business Job Protection Act) two distribution election changes in 457 plans. These plans could not commingle assets with other types of DC plans. It should come as little or no surprise that employers and providers have not focused their resources on retirees. As a result, employers and providers will require more preparations to deal with this group effectively. Curriculum in this area may include:

- **Asset allocation in retirement.** Longer life spans require different strategies for retirees than those developed even a couple of decades ago. Public sector retirees, especially safety and education retirees, often retire earlier and therefore can anticipate a longer retirement life.

  As discussed above, this demographic dynamic necessitates a change in how we think about retirees as DC plan participants. To be sure, they may no longer contribute to the employer plan but their accumulated asset size more often than not counterbalances this shortcoming. As a result, it is important to provide education to this group based on life expectancies and distribution needs. That education may include selection of investment choices (e.g., more aggressive asset classes) that have been traditionally ignored or discounted. As an example, a retiree who converts all assets to conservative investments may not serve his or her best interests if he or she lives for another 20 or 30 years because those investments may not even keep pace with inflationary increases.

- **Understanding distribution options.** This section as described for pre-retirees differs from the type of information that is necessary for retirees. Some employers or providers establish parameters for distribution changes that are more confining than the legislative changes.

  Where these restrictions exist, it is critical for retirees to understand their implications. More broadly, retirees would benefit from more detailed discussions of the array of distribution options, the pros and cons of each option and the importance of revisiting options as retirement objectives or circumstances change.

- **Evaluating alternate retirement options.** As mentioned above, the siphoning of employer DC assets to individual brokers and brokerage houses will continue until employers and/or providers develop neutral processes that allow retirees to evaluate the strengths and weaknesses of their possible actions long before they are approached to move their assets out of the plan and into an individual retirement account.

Despite the historical malaise and current inertia, there are numerous educational outreach efforts that could provide quick value for this group and attractive outcomes (i.e., retaining plan assets) for employers and providers alike. For starters, developing a comparison of employer net return and value of services compared with those offered by individual brokers should provide a solid base for discussions. Second, preparing questions, such as those offered in the Education Challenge: Self-Assessment Tool in Chapter 5.3, can readily be used by retirees to assess independently the value of employer services compared to individually provided benefits. Third, the overarching educational plan mentioned in Chapter 4.2 can disclose the types of outreach efforts to retirees that will confirm their ongoing importance to the plan well in advance of their retirement. If retirees understand that services will continue for them in much the same manner and frequency they experienced as employees, it will heighten the value they attribute to their employers and providers.

Topical Education

The changes introduced by legislative and regulatory actions represent an opportunity for employers and providers not only to inform individuals about the changes but also, of equal importance, to correlate those changes to the ways in which plan management has been reshaped. In fact, an effective overarching communication strategy would suggest that every new legislative or regulatory change creates a correlating opportunity to reinforce critical, ongoing educational themes important to the employer/provider and equally important to the plan participant.

For example, the Economic Growth and Tax Relief Reconciliation Act of 2001 (EGTRRA) increase in traditional and age 50-plus catch-up provisions dramatically expands the opportunities for older participants just as the tax credits open new opportunities for lower salaried employees. Providing information to these individuals accomplishes two simultaneous goals. It provides a contemporary update of the changes themselves and leads to a discussion of the broader retirement objectives that participants in all categories would do well to consider.

> *An effective overarching communication strategy would suggest that every new legislative or regulatory change creates a correlating opportunity to reinforce critical, ongoing educational themes important to the employer/provider and equally important to the plan participant.*

Employer or provider actions are also a gateway to similar discussions regarding broader subjects. For instance, employer revisions of investment policies or replacement of underperforming funds offer excellent opportunities to engage participants in meaningful forums on diversification and asset allocation and can yield numerous educational outcomes. By explaining to participants that plans have the fiduciary responsibility to review fund performance, utilize appropriate benchmarks and take appropriate action (which includes fund elimination or replacement), participants may also learn that they need to conduct, on an individual basis, a similar process for their own investments.

Conducting surveys and providing plan participants with the results of those surveys not only discloses how individuals are similar or different from their peer survey respondents, but it provides employers and providers the opportunity to evaluate the effectiveness of their educational efforts. It allows them to forecast upcoming changes and new modifications, and reinforce the more effective strategies participants can consider to be a successful investor.

> *It behooves an employer and provider to leverage these topical announcements into broader discussions that reinforce important themes and elevate participant knowledge.*

It behooves an employer and provider to leverage these topical announcements into broader discussions that reinforce important themes and elevate participant knowledge.

Conclusion

Part 4 began with an acknowledgment. It is fitting to close with one.

Education, while critical, is never easy. If it is possible to overlay a scientific principle on retirement education, the law of inertia seems apt. If it is possible to describe educational challenges with an adage, the ability to lead a horse to water but the inability to force it to drink seems appropriate.

Anyone who works in this field knows the ingrained characteristic of retirement planning. It is hard to get participants to invest, especially early. It is hard to motivate them to increase their investments. It has been historically difficult to get them to reevaluate their investments or reallocate/rebalance their portfolios regularly. It is an unending challenge to keep them engaged on behalf of their own interests.

> *Everyone can admit that participant education, true participant education, is an uphill struggle requiring persistence, creativity, incentives, rewards and an unflagging commitment. It is understandable in the face of these requirements that so much of what is marketed as education is merely window-dressing. Real education requires real resources and a focused dedication to using those resources again and again on behalf of participants.*

In short, everyone can admit that participant education, true participant education, is an uphill struggle requiring persistence, creativity, incentives, rewards and an unflagging commitment. It is understandable in the face of these requirements that so much of what is marketed as education is merely window dressing. Real education requires real resources and a focused dedication to using those resources again and again on behalf of participants.

The task is unending to be sure. There will always be new participants who need to learn from the ground up. There will always be market forces that play short-term havoc with even the best long-term individual retirement plan strategies. Precisely because the task is unending, success can appear elusive, unattainable and frankly too daunting to tackle.

> *When all is said and done, though, there is great satisfaction in the ceaseless pursuit, through education, of a more intelligent, self-interested investor.*

The French existentialist Albert Camus wrote a short story based on the Greek legend, *The Myth of Sisyphus.* Sisyphus was a Greek king condemned by the gods to an eternity of rolling a stone up a hill only to have it roll down again. The myth expressed the epitome of purposeless toil.

Who, in their right mind, would exchange places with Sisyphus? Who could possibly derive any satisfaction or happiness from endless work and no results? Camus, however, had a different insight and unearthed something of value even from this ostensibly bleak story. He argued throughout his story that the action itself had its own reward. He closed his short story with these words: "The struggle itself toward the heights is enough to fill a man's heart. One must imagine Sisyphus happy."

The educational efforts that employers and providers exert on behalf of plan participants are not purposeless, however frustrating. However daunting, the responsibility to educate employees to invest early and to make appropriate investment selections in a participant-directed investment benefit is real and serious and carries enormous consequences for participants and fiduciary decision makers alike.

When all is said and done, though, there is great satisfaction in the ceaseless pursuit, through education, of a more intelligent, self-interested investor.

PART 5

Appendix

Web Site Resources

The Web sites below provide an ongoing resource for identifying contemporary issues regarding deferred compensation/defined contribution (DC) legislative changes, alternative perspectives, plan documents and materials and other related information that is important to organizational practitioners as well as plan participants.

American Legislative Exchange Counsel (ALEC)—
> www.alec.org
>> ALEC is the nation's largest bipartisan, individual membership association of state legislators, with nearly 3,000 members.

American Savings Education Council (ASEC)—
> www.asec.org
>> ASEC is a coalition of private and public sector institutions that undertakes initiatives to raise public awareness about what is needed to ensure long-term personal financial independence.

American Society of Pension Actuaries (ASPA)—
> www.aspa.org
>> ASPA is a national organization of employee benefits professionals including pension actuaries, consultants, administrators, accountants, attorneys, chartered life underwriters and more.

Association of Private Pension & Welfare Plans (APPWP)—
www.appwp.org
> APPWP serves as an advocate of employer-sponsored benefit programs in Washington, D.C., and is comprised of major corporations, professionals in banking, finance, insurance, law, accounting, consulting and other fields providing service and support to corporate benefit plans.

Association of Public Pension Fund Auditors (APPFA)—
www.appfa.org
> APPFA is a nonprofit organization whose members are comprised predominantly of internal auditors of public employee retirement systems, including state, municipal and teacher plans.

BenefitsLink—
www.benefitslink.com
> A free nationwide (USA) Internet link to information and services for employers sponsoring employee benefit plans, companies providing products and services for plans and participating employees.

Defined Contribution and Participant Behavior Research Program—
www.ebri.org/DCproject/dc_program_fact_sheet.html

Defined Contribution News—
www.dcnews.com
> A biweekly newsletter providing tips, leads and inside intelligence on the DC market.

Employee Benefit Research Institute (EBRI)—
www.ebri.org
> EBRI is a nonprofit, nonpartisan organization committed to original public policy research and education on economic security and employee benefits.

ERISA Industry Committee (ERIC)—
www.eric.org
> ERIC is an association of America's largest employers committed to the advancement of voluntary retirement, health care coverage and other employee benefit plans.

Government Finance Officers Association (GFOA)—
www.gfoa.org
GFOA is the professional association of state/provincial and local finance officers in the United States and Canada.

International Foundation for Retirement Education (InFRE)—
www.infre.org
InFRE sets the standard for retirement-focused designations (Certified Retirement Counselor, Certified Retirement Administrator) for retirement professionals. These designations ensure that employees are getting assistance from individuals with a certification of competency, skill and experience to help employees plan for their retirement goals.

International Foundation of Employee Benefit Plans—
www.ifebp.org
The International Foundation is the largest educational association serving the employee benefits field.

Morningstar—
www.morningstar.com
Morningstar is a provider of mutual fund, stock and variable-insurance investment information.

National Association of Government Defined Contribution Administrators (NAGDCA)—
www.nagdca.org
NAGDCA's mission is to unite representatives from state and local governments along with private sector organizations that service and support DC plans by providing education and research initiatives and ongoing federal legislative involvement.

National Association of Public Pension Attorneys (NAPPA)—
www.nappa.org
NAPPA is a professional and educational organization for attorneys who represent public pension funds.

National Association of State Auditors, Comptrollers, and Treasurers (NASACT)—
www.sso.org/nasact/

NASACT acts as a representative of states' interests in financial management issues by providing leadership and training in meeting the increasingly complex challenges of professional state fiscal and financial management.

National Association of State Retirement Administrators (NASRA)—
www.nasra.org

NASRA is a nonprofit association comprised of the administrators of the state retirement systems for the 50 states, the District of Columbia, and the territories of American Samoa, Guam, Puerto Rico and the Virgin Islands.

National Commission on Retirement Policy—
www.csis.org/retire/

The mission of the retirement commission, a 24-member panel of bipartisan congressional and private sector members, is to better inform the public and policy makers on the need for comprehensive, bipartisan reforms on retirement security issues.

National Conference on Public Employee Retirement Systems (NCPERS)—
www.ncpers.org

NCPERS is an organization comprised of representatives of public employee retirement systems.

National Council on Teacher Retirement (NCTR)—
www.nctr.org

NCTR is an independent organization dedicated to safeguard the integrity of public retirement systems in the United States and in its territories to which teachers belong and to promote the rights and benefits of the members, present or future, of such systems.

National Defined Contribution Council (NDCC)—
www.gwami.com/ndcc.html

Formed specifically to address the needs and concerns of plan service providers, the NDCC is dedicated to the promotion and protection of the DC industry and the public it serves.

The Pension Research Council—
www.aspa.org
> The Pension Research Council of the Wharton School of the University of Pennsylvania is an organization committed to generating debate on key policy issues affecting pensions and other employee benefits.

Pensions & Investments—
www.pionline.com
> The international newspaper of the money management industry.

PLANSPONSOR—
www.assetpub.com
> PLANSPONSOR, the leading North American monthly magazine reporting on the pension industry, is geared to organizations sponsoring pension plans for their employees.

Profit Sharing/401(k) Council of America (PSCA)—
www.401k.org
> PSCA is a national, nonprofit association representing its members' interests to federal policymakers and offers assistance with profit-sharing and 401(k) plan design, administration, investment, compliance and communication.

Public Retirement Information Systems Management (PRISM)—
www.prism.ca.gov
> PRISM is an organization for management information systems directors of public retirement funds.

Public Retirement Institute (PRI)—
www.pripension.org
> PRI addresses issues of interest to the public pension industry through research on public-sector pension plans.

State and Local Pension Exchange—
www.pensionexchange.com
> A reference site with a goal of enhancing the availability and accessibility of public pension fund information for the public pension fund community, including fund managers, administrators, trustees, policy makers, members, professional service providers and other interested individuals and organizations.

Sample Policy

COMMUNICATION POLICY

The purpose of a communication policy is to establish the objectives decision makers identify in their delivery of information to plan participants and other stakeholders to assure that important information and education is provided and that plan participant actions are based upon informed decisions.

Purpose Statement

We recognize that plan participants must have access to clear, practical information about general plan parameters, their investment options and the consequences of their individual decisions.

Specific Commitments

To meet participant needs, we make the following commitments:

• We will provide accurate plan documents that clearly define eligibility, participant rights and options and, in general, govern the actions we take.

• We will provide summary plan descriptions that provide clear, unambiguous language regarding various options plan participants may elect.

• We have developed a broad educational program that will be delivered on a regular basis to all plan participants. This program will be available on a group and individual basis. Information will also be provided in print and through electronic media.

Sample Documents

DEFERRED COMPENSATION COMMITTEE MEMBER

MEMBER RESPONSIBILITIES—AGENDA

I. Organization of Committee
- Board Resolution Authorizing Committee
- Committee Representation/Selection Process
- List of Current Committee Members

II. Overview of 457 Deferred Compensation Plan
- Internal Revenue Code Section 457
- Review of Formal Plan Document
- Annual Maximums
- Current Providers
- Investment Options
- Current Enrollment/Fund Selection
- Provider Plan Documents

III. Investment Policy
- Review of Investment Policy
- Annual Performance Review
- Review of New Funds/Underperforming Funds

IV. Member Responsibilities—Fiduciary
- ERISA Section 404(c)
- Responsibility to Plan/Not Organization or Union
- Investment Due Diligence Review
- Other Special Responsibilities
- Contract Review
- Request for Proposal Responsibility

V. Member Responsibilities—Hardship Withdrawals
- Sample Hardship Withdrawal Application
- Taxability of Hardship Withdrawals
- Communication of Hardship Withdrawal Information to Participants
- Hardship Withdrawal Process
- Hardship Withdrawal Checklist

VI. Member Responsibilities—Meetings
- Periodic Meeting Schedule
- Attendance at Meetings—Expectations
- Meeting Minutes
- Staff Responsibilities
- Open to Public (California Brown Act)

VII. Member Responsibilities—Conflict of Interest
- State Conflict of Interest Provisions
- Annual Conflict of Interest Statement

VIII. Participant Informational Sessions
- • Frequency of Informational Sessions
- • Content of Informational Sessions
- • Basic Plan Parameters
- • Investment Selection Information/Resources
- • General Investment Strategies
- • Stage-of-Life Investment Strategies
- • Planning for Retirement
- • Distribution Options/Selection

IX. Legislative Changes/Regulations
- • Small Business Job Protection Act
- • Tax Reform Act
- • Omnibus Budget Reconciliation Act (1990)
- • 401(a) Plan for Seasonal, Temporary and Part-Time Employees
- • Economic Growth and Tax Relief Reconciliation Act (2001)

X. Strategic Issues
- • Prospective Legislation
- • Deferred Compensation/Defined Contribution Modifications
- • Employer Retirement Strategies

XI. Committee Member—Questions/Issues

CHECKLIST FOR RETIREES CONSIDERING ROLLOVER OF FUNDS TO OTHER ACCOUNTS

The following checklist is provided to assist you in your evaluation of whether to transfer funds from your employer 457 deferred compensation plan to another eligible plan or Individual Retirement Account (IRA). These transfers are now permissible because of the Economic Growth and Tax Relief Reconciliation Act of 2001. The transfer of funds is not, by itself, a taxable event when transferred directly from one plan to another. But there are many factors that should be considered before transferring funds. As an example, funds in 457 plans are not subject to distribution tax penalties if taken before the age of 59½. By contrast, 401(a), 401(k), 403(b) and IRAs **are subject to these penalties.** Also, once 457 funds are transferred to these other types of accounts they automatically and irrevocably become subject to distribution penalties before the age of 59½.

You have already received a formal, legal summary of the consequences of transferring funds to another account. The list below summarizes some of the questions or issues we encourage you to ask of the prospective plan administrator/broker of your new fund(s). For each question below we have also provided information on your incumbent plan for purposes of comparison.

CHECK ✔	CATEGORY— QUESTION/ISSUE	ADDITIONAL INFORMATION
	FUND PERFORMANCE	
	Are a broad, diverse variety of funds available to you in your new plan?	Current plans over numerous funds in each asset class to provide a variety both within and across asset classes to assure diversity based on individual preferences.
	Are funds regularly reviewed against appropriate bench-marks to determine ongoing fund performance?	Current plans provide annual fund performance analysis to assure that it remains competitive against its peer group. Under-performing funds are placed on probation and then eliminated if performance continues to be non-competitive.
	Who conducts the review of fund performance?	Fund managers, plan administrators, employers and sometimes-neutral third parties perform fund evaluation to assure due diligence regarding overall fund performance.
	Is fund performance analysis provided to you routinely?	Fund performance is evaluated annually and made available to all participants.
	Will your new provider review fund performance with you individually and recommend alternative/ diverse investments for your consideration?	Individuals may contact their representative to evaluate individual funds and overall portfolio mix to determine whether the investments are appropriately diversified, based on retirement objectives and risk tolerance. Investment information services from a neutral third party are also offered to assure that overall portfolio and individual investments are appropriate based on your objectives and needs.

CHECK ✔	CATEGORY— QUESTION/ISSUE	ADDITIONAL INFORMATION
	FUND FEES	
	Will your new plan provide information on **all** fees that are charged for your investments including: • Front end sales charges/loads? • Back-end sales charges/loads? • Deferred sales charges? • 12(b)(1), management fees? • Administrative (transactions based, account maintenance, reallocation or fund transfers)? • Have you compared them with your current investment provider?	All fees are made available to participants upon fund selection and are available thereafter upon request.
	Will your new plan put **in writing** a confirmation that **all fees** are disclosed?	**All** fees are disclosed to assure that there are no hidden charges that reduce net return to participant.

CHECK ✔	CATEGORY— QUESTION/ISSUE	ADDITIONAL INFORMATION
WITHDRAWAL CONSEQUENCES/AVAILABILITY OF FUNDS		
	How do you access your money with the new plan? What payment options will your new plan offer? What tax consequences affect the withdrawal?	Your current plan offers a variety of methods for withdrawing your money. You have access to retirement information that can provide you with illustrations of all methods of payment as well as the tax consequences of your withdrawal. You also have access to insurance based withdrawal options for guaranteeing payments over your life time and/or that of your spouse's. Your current plan also offers calculations of mandatory minimum distribution requirements.

CHECK ✔	CATEGORY— QUESTION/ISSUE	ADDITIONAL INFORMATION
	EDUCATIONAL SERVICES	
	Does your new plan provide ongoing information and education regarding fund options, investment information, evaluation, legislative changes, etc. to keep you informed?	Current providers offer year-around educational programs to summarize key legislative/legal changes. Additionally, individual appointments are provided to assure that individuals receive the kind of general information and specific fund information they need to make informed decisions.
	How will information be provided in your new plan?	Information is provided through a variety of resources. Quarterly newsletters keep you informed of topics of interest and important changes. Additionally, the providers and employer have Web site resources that provide access to broad information on latest trends, fund performance, self-assessment of risk, identification of risk tolerance, investment advice.
	How will I learn about important legislative changes or changes in the conditions of my investments?	Current providers offer a wide array of information that is specifically targeted to legislative and legal changes that may impact the amount you contribute and take in distribution, the options that are available to you and the impact those options have on your retirement decisions.

EDUCATION CHALLENGE: SELF-ASSESSMENT TOOL

Editor's note: This checklist is reprinted from pages 107-111 of Part 4 of this book for the convenience of readers who wish to copy and use it as a separate document.

With education, young employees **understand** the value of making contributions early and using the length of their career to amass sufficient resources for their retirement. They know that it is never too early to start and that the early contributions, even if small, produce greater results than larger contributions later. In a perhaps more poetic way, they avoid the chief shortcoming so eloquently voiced by Oscar Wilde in his *Picture of Dorian Grey,* "To get back one's youth, one has merely to repeat one's follies."

Do employers:

☐ Communicate to young employees how vital early contributions are?

☐ Target young employees with educational material that substantiates the enormous value of early contributions?

☐ Offer regular training to demonstrate these values?

☐ Use incentives to increase young employee participation?

☐ Monitor the number of participants by age?

☐ Assess where communication and education efforts might be most successful?

With education, participants **understand** that they must know themselves and their financial needs and objectives for investment strategies to work. They must know how tolerant they are of risk. They must have a general idea of when they plan to retire, and they must have some rudimentary sense of what they think they need to retire satisfactorily and successfully. Perhaps most importantly, they must be able to correlate their knowledge with broad-based factual information regarding retirement trends and population-based information to assure that their individual expectations are in line with established characteristics.

Do employers:

- ☐ Utilize self-assessment tools that allow participants to determine their risk tolerance, retirement objectives and time horizon?

- ☐ Make these tools accessible and provide guidance on how participants may use the tools to evaluate their individual needs and preferences?

- ☐ Identify methods to promote their use by all plan participants?

- ☐ Measure the success of their efforts?

With education, participants **understand** that the strategies to build their retirement savings can change or evolve during their life and that such change and evolution requires that they revisit their objectives and strategies regularly. They use these self-assessments to rebalance their portfolios and adjust their overall retirement objectives and expectations.

Do employers:

- ☐ Develop training programs that identify how investment strategies may change over the career of an individual based on marriage, birth, divorce and other family status changes?

- ☐ Target life cycle training to individuals to capture the changing needs of participants at different times in their careers?

- ☐ Measure the ways in which individuals should modify their investments as they age and approach retirement?

With education, participants **understand** that their selection of investments and the allocation of contributions to each investment type is the optimal way to achieve their retirement objectives. They know that pursuing "hot investments" and the "fund du jour" will thwart their aims. They know that the opposite strategy of investing in fixed account or stable value funds throughout their career will lead to an ongoing erosion of retirement assets. Somehow, they must understand and overcome the inherent disadvantage in Mark Twain's spurious advice: "October. This is one of the peculiarly dangerous months to speculate in stocks. The others are July, January, September, April, November, May, March, June, December, August and February."

Do employers:

- ☐ Unshackle participants of the notion that their success is not improved by pursuing a particular fund or fund category but by having participants understand the value of asset allocation over fund selection?

- ☐ Demonstrate their confidence in replacing underperforming funds, however popular, with the knowledge that their participants understand and accept the change?

- ☐ Develop programs to educate participants about the historical failure of individuals who "time the market" or follow hot funds?

With education, participants **understand** that a proper evaluation of retirement resources must include all resources, their own and their spouses', to be thoughtfully balanced. They expect to include in any self-assessment the DC sources as well as employer defined benefit (DB) plan payments, Social Security income, other outside resources and, where appropriate, spousal resources.

Do employers:

- ☐ Structure their self-assessment programs to allow employees to incorporate all sources of retirement income?

- ☐ Provide guidance to employees in how to structure portfolios based on the total sources of potential retirement income?

- ☐ Use tools that allow participants to incorporate outside assets in their portfolio assumptions and wealth accumulation projections?

- ☐ Collaborate with internal DB providers to coordinate DB/DC resources into a single model that participants can understand and easily use?

- ☐ Establish specific expectations as to how these tools will be promoted to assure maximum use?

With education, participants **understand** that changes in career are not opportunities to liberate funds for immediate purposes, however compelling the purpose, even, for instance, the purchase of a home. They know a commitment to retirement requires a disciplined commitment to contributing and an equally disciplined commitment to maintaining assets intact for retirement.

Do employers:

☐ Develop programs to provide exiting employees with information regarding the importance of retaining their retirement assets?

☐ Discuss with incoming employees the value of transferring into employer programs existing assets that are located elsewhere?

☐ Assure that terminated employees receive the same information and educational opportunities that active and retired employee participants enjoy?

With education, lower salaried employees, especially single parent employees, **understand** that their circumstances are not a prohibition to participate but a challenge. It's a challenge that can be overcome using the knowledge they can gain regarding financial resource management and tax advantages. Women, in particular, recognize that precisely because they have traditionally lower salaries than men and longer life expectancies after retirement, these contributions are more critical for retirement security.

Do employers:

☐ Target outreach efforts to lower salaried workers and customize programs to acknowledge the greater difficulty and importance of these individuals contributing to a DC program?

☐ Focus on tax advantages for lower income participants?

☐ Integrate DC contributions in the larger context of overall financial planning strategies for these individuals?

With education, participants **understand** that their proximity to retirement requires special review and consideration. They need to be aware that longer life spans may require ongoing long-term commitment and not massive overhaul of investment strategy.

Do employers:

☐ Incorporate DC objectives in financial planning and preretirement seminars to highlight the value of catch-up provisions, rebalancing, reassessing retirement objectives?

☐ Meet with retirees or preretirees on a regular basis?

☐ Incorporate information about life expectancy and the impact on retirement assets?

With education, retirees **understand** that they are unlikely to find competitive offers, in either investment support or general education, through individual brokers or companies, however tempting and however familiar and friendly their relationships with individual brokers. They recognize that these companies and their employees are investing substantial amounts in marketing campaigns to attract individual, high-asset participants and that this marketing barrage does not mean that they provide a superior investment or better services.

Do employers:

☐ Assess the number of retirees and the amount of assets being "lost" from employer plans as a result of migration to individual brokers?

☐ Offer information or education regarding rollover considerations to counteract the significant marketing campaign undertaken by companies in the wake of the new portability afforded as a result of the Economic Growth and Tax Relief Reconciliation Act (EGTRRA)?

☐ Provide retirees with the tools to evaluate both the advantages and disadvantages of transferring funds to individual retirement accounts?

☐ Offer counseling programs in recognition that retirees are still customers and still deserve the continued educational services to help them make informed decisions throughout their retirement years?

SAMPLE PERFORMANCE STANDARDS/GUARANTEES

Below is a list of performance standards, dates and guaranteed amounts for proposed services. For each service, the date will represent the date service will be provided. For each service, the guarantee will be the amount of dollars payable if the standard is not met by the specified time.

Respondents will confirm their acceptance of the standard (as well as date and guarantee amount) by checking "will meet." If respondent is "unable to meet" the standard, date or guarantee or chooses to "exceed" the standard, an explanation and proposed alternative standard/date/guarantee must be provided.

Performance standards will be measured by mutually agreeable criteria. Where information regarding service performance is measured by the provider, provider must propose a specific method/criteria for assessing compliance to standard.

1. TRANSITION SERVICES **(PERIOD FROM FORMAL APPROVAL TO FUND TRANSITION)**	
Pre-Transition Services Standard: Assure attendance at finalist meetings by representatives who will provide direct transition and ongoing services. **Date:** Finalist Meeting **Guarantee:** N/A	☐ Will meet ☐ Unable to meet ☐ Will exceed
Standard: Answer phone calls from Plan Sponsor contact designee within 24 hours *and* propose method of measuring standard. **Date:** Transition Period. **Guarantee:** $100 per incident for failure to return phone calls from Plan Sponsor contact designee within 24 hours.	☐ Will meet ☐ Unable to meet ☐ Will exceed
Standard: Provide draft, customized contract (incorporating agreed-upon, proposed services). **Date:** 30 Days after formal approval by Plan Sponsor. **Guarantee:** $1,000	☐ Will meet ☐ Unable to meet ☐ Will exceed
Standard: Respond, in writing with a copy to Plan Sponsor, to phone or in-person complaints within 5 business days. **Date:** Transition Period. **Guarantee:** $100 per incident of failure to respond to complaint within specified time.	☐ Will meet ☐ Unable to meet ☐ Will exceed
Standard: Comply with Sarbanes-Oxley Act requirements regarding notification of blackout period. **Date:** Transition Period. **Guarantee:** $1,000 plus the equivalent of any penalties that would be assessed.	☐ Will meet ☐ Unable to meet ☐ Will exceed
Standard: Finalize and publish performance standards and guarantees. **Date:** Provide final copy to Plan Sponsor within 30 days of being selected by Plan Sponsor. **Guarantee:** $500	☐ Will meet ☐ Unable to meet ☐ Will exceed
Standard: Provided agreed-upon training to employees and retirees within transition period. **Date:** Transition Period. **Guarantee:** $1,000	☐ Will meet ☐ Unable to meet ☐ Will exceed

2. TRANSITION EXIT (PERIOD FROM NOTIFICATION OF NON-RENEWAL TO FUND TRANSITION)	
Standard: Upon termination, provide: (1) last four quarters of transaction reports, (2) current account balances, (3) past 12 months distribution and deferral information and (4) loan or other outstanding payment amounts. **Date:** Within 30 business days after termination notification, provide report on disk, tape or Internet. **Guarantee:** $1,000 for initial failure to provide and $500 per day thereafter.	☐ Will meet ☐ Unable to meet ☐ Will exceed
Standard: Upon termination, provide information as described in Section 8 on disk, tape or Internet. **Date:** Within 30 days of request. **Guarantee:** $1,000 on failure to provide information within timeframe.	☐ Will meet ☐ Unable to meet ☐ Will exceed

3. CUSTOMER SERVICES	
Standard: Telephone calls to service center(s) will be answered within 90 seconds 90% of the time. (Propose method of measuring standard.) **Date:** Quarterly summary/review due before the end of the month following the quarter. **Guarantee:** $1,000 per year for failure to meet annual, calendar year average.	☐ Will meet ☐ Unable to meet ☐ Will exceed
Standard: Participant statements will be mailed within 10 business days after quarter-end. **Date:** Quarterly. **Guarantee:** $5 per participant per quarter for each statement postmarked after 10 business days.	☐ Will meet ☐ Unable to meet ☐ Will exceed
Standard: Finalize customized Web within parameters specified in 5.2B site providing hot link between Plan Sponsor and provider Web sites and draft participant communication advertising site content and way to access. **Date:** Due by 3rd month after implementation. **Guarantee:** $500 for failure to provide live Web site and participant announcement by end of 3rd month after implementation.	☐ Will meet ☐ Unable to meet ☐ Will exceed
Standard: Process investment fund transfers, contribution reconciliation and posting within one business day and propose method of measuring standard. **Date:** Annual report due 31 days after each 12-month period from fund transition. **Guarantee:** Maximum $1,000 for failure to meet agreed-upon standard.	☐ Will meet ☐ Unable to meet ☐ Will exceed
Standard: Process hardship distributions, rollover requests, in-service distributions, retiree distribution requests within 5 working days of acceptable documentation and propose method of measuring standard. **Date:** Annual summary of performance by provider. **Guarantee:** $1,000 annually for failure to meet standard in 90% of actions.	☐ Will meet ☐ Unable to meet ☐ Will exceed

3. CUSTOMER SERVICES (Continued)	
Standard: Review plan documents for legal, legislative compliance, identify policy issues between Plan Sponsor and provider and summarize, in writing, any recommended changes to documents. **Date:** Within 180 days of transition and annually thereafter. **Guarantee:** $500 for failure to provide each written summary.	☐ Will meet ☐ Unable to meet ☐ Will exceed
Standard: Review investment policy and summarize, in writing, any recommended changes. **Date:** Annually with fund evaluation results. **Guarantee:** $500 for failure to provide review/summary within specified timeframe.	☐ Will meet ☐ Unable to meet ☐ Will exceed
Standard: Provide written proposal of services and draft plan for ongoing participant communication utilizing Internet educational resources (e.g., internet or computer-based training). **Date:** Within 180 days of fund transition. **Guarantee:** $500 for failure to provide proposal within timeframe.	☐ Will meet ☐ Unable to meet ☐ Will exceed

4. REPORTS	
Standard: Provide written summary of quarterly reports to Plan Sponsor. **Date:** Mailed within 30 days of quarter-end. **Guarantee:** $500 per failure to provide reports by specified date.	☐ Will meet ☐ Unable to meet ☐ Will exceed
Standard: Provide written draft proposal for recommended reports that will be available to Plan Sponsor online (Internet) including proposed access protocols. **Date:** Within 90 days of fund transition. **Guarantee:** $500 for failure to provide written draft proposal within specified time.	☐ Will meet ☐ Unable to meet ☐ Will exceed
Standard: Conduct training of Plan Sponsor-designated personnel on access to online reports and use of reporting capability. **Date:** Within 120 days of fund transition. **Guarantee:** $500 for failure to provide training within specified time.	☐ Will meet ☐ Unable to meet ☐ Will exceed

5. SURVEYS	
Standard: Draft satisfaction survey. **Date:** Draft due by end of 4th month after implementation. **Guarantee:** $500 if failure to provide draft survey.	☐ Will meet ☐ Unable to meet ☐ Will exceed
Standard: Distribute survey to all plan participants. **Date:** Distribution by end of 6th month after implementation. **Guarantee:** $500 if failure to mail 30 days from date of final agreed-upon survey content.	☐ Will meet ☐ Unable to meet ☐ Will exceed
Standard: Analyze survey results, provide executive summary and recommended actions. **Date:** Complete by end of 8th month after implementation. **Guarantee:** $1,000 if Executive Summary and recommended actions are not received within time period.	☐ Will meet ☐ Unable to meet ☐ Will exceed
Standard: Repeat survey process steps described above for surveys at 24 and 36 months after implementation. **Date:** Executive Summary and Recommended Actions due by end of 24th and 36th month after implementation. **Guarantee:** $1,000 for failure to provide Executive Summary and Recommended Actions by 24th and 36th month.	☐ Will meet ☐ Unable to meet ☐ Will exceed
Standard: Survey results will average Satisfactory or Above and will be incorporated into Executive Summary and Recommended Actions document. **Date:** Due by 8th, 24th and 36th month after implementation. **Guarantee:** $1,000 for any survey results that fail to meet Satisfactory or Above.	☐ Will meet ☐ Unable to meet ☐ Will exceed

6. EDUCATIONAL SERVICES	
Standard: Provide training to all decision-makers and administrative staff on 404(c) requirements. **Date:** 90 days after fund transition. **Guarantee:** $500 for failure to provide on-site training within timeframe.	☐ Will meet ☐ Unable to meet ☐ Will exceed
Standard: Propose and schedule first year on-site training sessions and content of training for decision-makers and administrative personnel. **Date:** Proposal within 90 days after fund transition and educational programs quarterly thereafter. **Guarantee:** $500 for failure to provide proposed training and $500 for failure to provide four training sessions in any year of contract.	☐ Will meet ☐ Unable to meet ☐ Will exceed
Standard: Develop and schedule new decision-maker training for Plan Sponsor-identified new Committee members or administrative staff. **Date:** Provide half-day on-site training for identified new personnel within 30 days of notification by Plan Sponsor. **Guarantee:** $500 for failure to provide training within specified timeframe.	☐ Will meet ☐ Unable to meet ☐ Will exceed
Standard: After implementation, provide mutually agreeable number of educational seminars annually on site to participants. **Date:** Within 90 days after fund transition. **Guarantee:** $1,000 for failure to provide agreed-upon number of on-site group seminars.	☐ Will meet ☐ Unable to meet ☐ Will exceed
Standard: After implementation, provide newsletters to plan participants regarding plan benefits/issues. **Date:** Quarterly. **Guarantee:** Annual $500 penalty for failure to provide quarterly newsletters.	☐ Will meet ☐ Unable to meet ☐ Will exceed
Standard: Provide representative on site for mutually agreeable number of days per month/quarter/annual period to meet with plan participants. **Date:** Monthly/Quarterly/Annually. **Guarantee:** $1,000 per year if agreed-upon number of days is not provided.	☐ Will meet ☐ Unable to meet ☐ Will exceed

6. EDUCATIONAL SERVICES (Continued)

Standard: Provide draft PowerPoint and/or other communication material for transition specifically proposed for group meetings. Provide separate samples for employees/retirees. **Date:** 30 days after formal approval. **Guarantee:** $500 for initial failure to provide within 30 days.	☐ Will meet ☐ Unable to meet ☐ Will exceed
Standard: Draft communication to plan participants describing investment advice services and access. **Date:** Within 60 days of fund transition. **Guarantee:** $500 for initial failure to provide within 60 days after formal approval.	☐ Will meet ☐ Unable to meet ☐ Will exceed
Standard: Recommend, in writing, steps provider and Plan Sponsor may take to communicate and coordinate information regarding retirement benefits offered through the Plan Sponsor and available fund options. **Date:** Within 180 days of fund transition. **Guarantee:** $1,000 for failure to provide within specified time.	☐ Will meet ☐ Unable to meet ☐ Will exceed
Standard: Provide one half-day session per quarter/ semi-annual/annual to Plan Sponsor decision-making and administrative personnel on mutually agreeable topics. **Date:** Quarterly. **Guarantee:** $250 per quarter if education session is not provided.	☐ Will meet ☐ Unable to meet ☐ Will exceed

7. MISCELLANEOUS PERFORMANCE STANDARDS/GUARANTEES	
Standard: Provide Web site copy listing final agreed-upon Performance Standards/Guarantees. **Date:** Implementation Date and 30 days after any mutually agreed-upon revisions. **Guarantee:** $500 for each failure to provide Web-ready document to Plan Sponsor.	☐ Will meet ☐ Unable to meet ☐ Will exceed
Standard: Provide agreed-upon number of written copies of final agreed-upon Performance Standards/Guarantees to Plan Sponsor for distribution. **Date:** Implementation Date and 30 days after any mutually agreed-upon revisions. **Guarantee:** $500 for each failure to provide specified number of copies of final agreed-upon Performance Standards/Guarantees.	☐ Will meet ☐ Unable to meet ☐ Will exceed
Standard: Provide annual written summary of all Performance Standards/Guarantees categories and results to Plan Sponsor and as a Web document for communication to plan participants. **Date:** 30 days after annual anniversary of implementation. **Guarantee:** $1,000 for failure to provide Web-ready document within specified timeframe.	☐ Will meet ☐ Unable to meet ☐ Will exceed
Standard: Recommend, in writing, to Plan Sponsor any modifications/enhancements to Performance Standards/Guarantees. **Date:** 30 days after annual anniversary of implementation. **Guarantee:** $1,000 for failure to provide written recommendations.	☐ Will meet ☐ Unable to meet ☐ Will exceed

INDEX